Race, Rock & Religion

Race, Rock & Religion

Profiles From A Southern Journalist

Frye Gaillard

The East Woods Press

Library of Congress Cataloging in Publication Data

Gaillard, Frye, 1946-
    Race, rock, and religion.

    1. Southern States—Civilization—20th century. 2. Southern
States—Popular culture. 3. Southern States—Biography.
I. Title.

F216.2.G34 1982 975′.043 82-11325
ISBN 0-914788-59-0

Cover design by Kenn Compton

Cover photograph of Martin Luther King courtesy of the Martin
    Luther King Center
All other photographs courtesy of the *Charlotte Observer*, the
    Charlotte News and Knight Publishing Company

Typography by Raven Type
Printed in the United States of America

An East Woods Press Book
Fast & McMillan Publishers, Inc.
429 East Boulevard
Charlotte, N.C. 28203

For Rachel and Tracy

Acknowledgments

In 1981, I spent a year as writer-in-residence at Queens College in Charlotte, N.C. The idea for this book came out of conversations between Queens' energetic president, Billy Wireman, and me. I am grateful to Dr. Wireman for the interest and support he has provided this project.

I am also grateful to my editor, Rich Oppel, at the *Charlotte Observer*, who was similarly supportive. Most of the chapters that follow first appeared in the *Observer*, though parts of the book also appeared in the *Race Relations Reporter, Southern Voices, Parade, New West* and *Tar Heel Magazine*. Portions of two chapters appeared in different form in my first book, *Watermelon Wine: The Spirit of Country Music*.

I received considerable support and encouragement along the way, particularly from my editors at East Woods Press, Linda Benefield and Sally McMillan, who helped transform a hodge-podge collection into a coherent whole, and from my *Charlotte Observer* colleague and friend, Lisa Hammersly, who read the whole manuscript and offered good suggestions.

I am grateful to all of them—but most of all I am grateful to the subjects of this book, people like Will Campbell, George Hamilton IV or Billy Graham, whose lives and talents have made this part of the country so distinctive.

Contents

Introduction

Though I didn't know it at the time, this book began about 15 years ago, when I graduated from college with a degree in history, returned home to Mobile, Ala., and took a job as a reporter for the Mobile Press Register. I soon discovered that I had changed some in college, for I had been there during the turmoil of the 1960s and had spent time on occasion with people like Tom Hayden, Robert Kennedy and Martin Luther King—all of whom, though discernibly different in their philosophies, represented an affront to the Deep South truisms on which I was raised.

What I experienced, therefore, when I returned to Mobile was a jarring case of culture shock, a collision between my newfound values, which were fraught with adolescent passion, and the lingering melodrama of life in the South. I became over the years a kind of Southern junkie, part voyeur, part chauvinist, part bleeding-heart critic, writing about the region from a number of vantage points.

I began by covering the civil rights movement—the ongoing upheavals over the question of black and white—which succeeded only partially, but changed the South more than anyone could have dreamed. I developed a little later a fascination with religion, initially because of its connection to civil rights. (Martin Luther King was much more a Baptist than a disciple of Ghandi.) But eventually, I became intrigued with Christianity *per se*—the startlingly simple notion that the life and death of Jesus still matter today, and perhaps more than anything else.

And finally, there was music, the folk rhythms of the region: rock, country, blues, the old-fashioned ballads of the Carolina hills. I began to feel that we are often too political in the writing of our history—that the music of Elvis Presley, Willie Nelson and a great many others reveals as much about us as elections and wars or marches in the streets.

So this book is a collection of journalism in which these themes interweave and overlap. The assumption is that the South's music, religion and anguished racial passage all offer glimpses into the Southern heart and soul. This is not, however, a systematic study. Each of the chapters was written to stand alone. Most first appeared in newspapers (a few in magazines) and were written in response to specific news events.

The result is a compendium of stories about some interesting people: Billy Graham, Elvis Presley, Martin Luther King and others less famous, whose triumphs, tragedies and choices in life are worthy of contemplation by the rest of us. I begin with King, perhaps the most eloquent of Southerners, whom I never understood until well after he was dead.

CHAPTER 1

A Dream Remembered:
Martin Luther King

October, 1977

As the cameras whirred, the summer sun beamed through the windows of the bus, driving the temperature well above 100. A burly, sweat-drenched good ol' boy, dressed as a Montgomery cop, ambled down the aisle—aiming himself toward a stony-faced black woman who had refused, moments before, to give up her seat.

"Didn't the driver tell you to get up?" the policeman demanded. His baleful eyes and even-toned voice suggested it wasn't a duty he performed with relish—that he possessed, like so many of his fellow Alabamians, a peculiar, unconscious ambivalence toward the habits of the day.

But habits are habits, and we quickly learned in Southern Alabama to keep any doubts or moral qualms tucked well below the surface. "Are you gonna get up?" the policeman demanded again.

The young woman looked up and answered in a tired but dignified voice, a faint trace of anxiety tugging at the edges. "Do you think I should have to give up my seat once I'm already on the bus?"

"I don't know," said the policeman, shuffling his feet in momentary confusion. "But the law is the law. You're under arrest." He nudged her gently up the aisle, as a voice from the back of the bus—loud and harsh, with accents foreign to the region—yanked us back into 1977. "Okay, cut," the voice affirmed with a nasal twang. "It's a take."

It was an eerie combination of reality and deja vu as director Abby Mann and his cast—Cicely Tyson, Paul Winfield and others—gathered to shoot a five-hour television movie on Martin Luther King. The site of the filming was Macon, Ga., not Montgomery, Ala., and there were constant technical intrusions— cameras, lights and the occasional cursings of sound men—to remind you it was only a movie.

And yet it was easy somehow to lose sight of all that, to find yourself carried back to a time not far in the past when the nation as a whole—and the South in particular—played out a bizarre and brutal melodrama. The real-life characters seem peculiar today in their unreality. Bull Conner is dead, Jim Clark is no longer a sheriff, and even George Wallace has been compelled by events to soften his line. But progress is relative, and the people who cracked open skulls at the Edmund Pettus bridge or turned their dynamite on four little girls in Birmingham aren't the products of an ancient time.

Abby Mann's thought-provoking film captures that fact with understated eloquence, and it was almost certain to generate painful feelings and a storm of controversy. Even before filming was completed, black leaders such as Jesse Jackson and Ralph David Abernathy charged that the script overstated King's limitations and gave too little credit to some key lieutenants, including themselves.

Those things may be important to Abernathy and Jackson, but for most Americans—those outside King's inner circle—the film should have a far different impact. Whatever its flaws, it offers a jolting reminder of how it was 22 years ago when Rosa Parks—a respected leader in the local NAACP—refused to relinquish her seat on a Montgomery bus.

I was 8 years old at the time. I'm 30 now, and like most Southern whites of my generation, my life has been altered immensely by that event and the movement it spawned. I was raised in Alabama with all the prevailing assumptions of white supremacy. Eventually, however, I changed with the region and became a civil rights reporter for several Southern newspapers and magazines. It was in that capacity that I arrived in Macon on a muggy July morning to watch the filming of Abby Mann's *King*.

The first scene I witnessed was the Rosa Parks arrest, and of all the episodes in the movie, it was the one I didn't want to miss. I've never understood the delicate psychological intertwinings of the movement's early days—what combination of desperation and foolhardy courage it must have taken to challenge a system in which whites controlled, as gently as possible, but as harshly as necessary, every conceivable institution of power.

Later, I could understand it, once the 1960s arrived and brought with them a we-shall-overcome momentum—a sense of inevitability for a cause that was totally just. But when Rosa Parks refused to give up her seat, and when a 26-year-old middle-class preacher named Martin Luther King sought to generate a mass movement in response, there was no reason whatsoever to believe it would work.

Those were the days when whites had unlimited access to the instruments of intimidation—beatings, killings and economic pressure—with no fear of reprisal.

14

I wanted to see how Abby Mann would deal with all that, and to improve my vantage point, I wrangled a bit part as a white bus rider and settled back to watch history re-enacted. During a lull, as camera tripods were set in place and technicians taped up microphones, I began idly perusing a press list of the cast. I discovered that Rosa Parks was being portrayed by a 22-year-old drama student named Yolanda King—Martin Luther King's oldest daughter, who was a bouncing, 10-pound baby in 1955, at the time Mrs. Parks was dragged off to jail.

The day after her scene was filmed, Yolanda King and I settled ourselves beside a second-floor swimming pool at the Macon Hilton and began a leisurely, meandering conversation about our respective Alabama childhoods. I told her about my grandfather—a prominent lawyer who had written, the year after the Montgomery bus boycott, a defense of white supremacy, published in the journal of the Alabama Bar Association.

I offered the anecdote with a sense of irony rather than shame, for I knew my grandfather well—knew, for example, that he was a gentle and decent man, incapable of dealing unkindly with anyone.

Yolanda listened quietly, a smile tugging at the corners of her mouth. She is an attractive young woman, with her mother's high, handsome cheekbones, but with her father's sad and steady eyes that seem to stare straight through to the heart of an issue.

"Daddy always believed," she explained softly, "that even on an individual level, prejudice was something conditioned into people, the product of beliefs held all their lives."

She explained that her father had that deeply Christian, even fundamentalist, ability to separate the sin from the sinner—to see bigotry and hatred not as outgrowths of some deep-seated Caucasian evil, but rather as inevitable by-products of a tainted culture. And so, even after the firehoses and attack dogs were unleashed in Birmingham, King could still make his dramatic appeals to conscience—holding out the olive branch to what he called "our misguided white brothers."

It was, of course, a rhetorical stance of immense utility, especially in the days when the movement's goal was to generate sympathy and support from the national press, the federal government and all the other outside forces whose pressure was essential if the South was to change.

But Yolanda King believes, in addition, that her father was giving voice to something blacks in the South had understood for years. It was the final bastion of dignity and grace, King believed, to understand your oppressor better than he understood you—to grasp instinctively the human compatibility of decency and meanness, and to see whites, therefore, as the servants rather than the masters of their own tragic flaws.

King had the ability to tap that understanding, injecting radical notions of equality and eye-to-eye brotherhood. It was, to say the least, a volatile chemistry in the segregated South—calling up, in the short run, the ugliest instincts that whites had to offer.

Yolanda King remembers, even from her girlhood days, that her father had no illusions about how ugly things might get. "He knew what kind of struggle it would be," she said. But King also recognized that the vicious resistance to the black drive for power had to be confronted and beaten on its own terms—that whites would never take him seriously until he proved that he didn't plan to lose.

All of that, however, generated enormous moral agonies and painful self-doubts. King was susceptible, Yolanda admits, to the most frequent criticism that came his way—i.e., that his non-violent stance was at bottom a mockery, designed to generate a violent response, strong enough to shake the status quo to its very foundation. Though the critique was almost always offered by defenders of segregation—people who didn't seem offended by violence itself—King recognized a grain of truth. It bothered him, and particularly so when people got hurt.

"Daddy firmly believed that suffering was redemptive," Yolanda explained, as she gazed at a dozen or so blacks and whites splashing in the motel pool. But King was jolted to the core, she said, when the movement's worst tragedies struck—especially the one on Sept. 15, 1963.

It had been a balmy, late summer's day in Birmingham, full of singing birds and the happy sounds of children on their way to Sunday School. At 10:29, however, 14 sticks of dynamite ripped through the back wall of the 16th Street Baptist Church—a sturdy brick edifice on the north side of Birmingham, where Martin Luther King conducted rallies during frequent trips to the city.

King was home in Atlanta when the explosion occurred, but it wasn't long before the phone call came, bringing with it the grisly details. At the time of the blast, four little girls, only a few years older than Yolanda, had made their way to the church's bottom-floor rest room. It was to be a special day for Cynthia Wesley, Denise McNair, Addie Mae Collins and Carol Robertson—a day when they and other junior high school students were to participate in the adult services.

In order to primp for the occasion, the girls had stopped by the rest room on their way from Sunday School to the main sanctuary. Nobody knows what happened next, but when the bomb exploded, the children collapsed in a mutilated heap, and the outer wall of the building fell in upon them. King would soon hear from 16th Street's pastor, John H. Cross, the story of how he and a civil defense team dug through the rubble, terrified at what they would find, and how even before they had reached the bodies, Denise McNair's grandfather had discovered a patent leather shoe lying among the bricks.

"He picked it up," John Cross would remember, "and as the tears streamed down his face, he said, 'That's Denise's shoe.' I told him, 'Mr. Pippin, that could be anybody's shoe. A lot of little girls wear shoes like that.' But of course he knew."

Yolanda King was only 8 years old at the time, but she remembers being deeply struck by her father's depression. Later, she would try to sort out the pieces—the bloody, soul-numbing collision in his head between the just and lofty rhetoric of liberation and the specter of four murdered children in a Birmingham church.

But fortunately for King, he was, above all else, a Baptist preacher—able to reach back in such times to the moral grounding that would keep him on course. He went to Birmingham to preach the eulogy, and this is what he said:

"History has proven over and over again that unmerited suffering is redemptive . . . so in spite of the darkness of this hour, we must not despair. We must not become bitter, nor must we harbor the desire to retaliate with violence. We must not lose faith in our white brothers. Somehow we must believe that even the most misguided among them can learn to respect the dignity and worth of all human personalities."

Paul Winfield, who plays King in Abby Mann's movie, delivers such speeches with remarkable credibility and power. The experience of seeing the words re-created on film, and hearing Yolanda King talk about the feelings behind them, combined to give the past a human dimension I had never really grasped.

It stirred, I suppose, the emotional voyeurism inside all reporters. But there was something else. I found myself moved again by events so familiar I had long since taken them for granted. I decided the next day to strike out for Birmingham, hoping to burrow beneath the glib martyrdom and sanctification surrounding King's memory.

Birmingham today is a sleek and progressive place, with glass-framed skyscrapers, six-lane interstates, and a spirit far removed from the days of Bull Connor.

I remember those days fairly well, for it was in Birmingham, sometime around 1962, that I first saw Martin Luther King. He was one of a handful of blacks being hauled toward a paddy wagon after attempting a lunch counter sit-in. I had arrived late, with no ambitions beyond a hamburger, and what stands out now is how unhistoric the whole occasion seemed.

I do remember feeling a brief and surprising flash of sympathy as I caught the expression on King's face—no trace of fear, or even resentment, as the policemen shoved him toward the car; just a steady-looking stoicism that.seemed to shade toward sadness.

It seemed clear who the underdog was, and yet I was shocked enough at my own compassion that I didn't confess it to my companions. Indignation quickly followed, and then dismissal, for those were the days before we took it seriously—when King's goals seemed so distant and peculiar that we didn't even bother with being very angry.

Fifteen years and a revolution later, the episode flashed through my mind as I headed for the Sixth Avenue Baptist Church, with its manicured lawn and an expensive dark-brick exterior that fits in well with Birmingham's decor.

"The Lord's been good to us," offered Rev. John Porter, smiling and munching away on a handful of Oreo cookies. He was sitting behind a glass desk in his posh inner office, dressed in a three-piece suit and looking for all the world like the caricature of a black Baptist preacher.

But outward appearances are deceiving; John Porter has been, for years, a savvy and candid civil rights leader, and more recently, a successful politician. In 1977, he became the first black appointed to the Alabama Board of Pardons and Paroles—a potentially important post in a state where prison populations are more than 60 percent black.

Porter, however, talked little about himself. Instead, we shifted the subject to 1963 and how he offered his church for the eulogy of the four murdered girls. He remembered the essence, but not the details of King's remarks that day—primarily, he concluded, because they were pretty much what he expected.

Porter knew King well—not as an intimate friend, for despite a pastor's one-to-one warmth, King kept his emotional distance from almost everyone (except perhaps his family, Ralph Abernathy, and one or two other associates.) But Porter was close enough to develop a fascination for King's complex character —and also to catch a glimpse of its foibles and limitations.

"I remember one time," he said, "when we were having some demonstrations and Dr. King came in and said very urgently, 'The press is losing interest, we've gotta do something to get their attention again.' Well, I thought to myself, 'we're supposed to be following the Constitution. We've got God on our side, we don't need the press.' But of course," Porter concluded, laughing at his own naivete, "he was right."

But if King, like other mortals, had his capacity for pragmatism (as well as fear, self-doubt, sexual longings and occasional arrogance), Porter believes he was, at bottom, exactly what he seemed to be. "He was a great preacher," Porter said. "It sounds simple, but he was his father's son. That is the key thing you have to understand."

Porter began a blunt testimonial on the influence of Martin Luther

King Sr., chuckling with mingled amusement and admiration. "The old man," he said, "was a bitter pill to swallow. Most people couldn't take him. I know I had a lot of trouble myself. But if you could get him down, he would do you good."

Through sheer force of personality, Porter explained, the older King made a deep impression on his son's religious views. King Sr. believed, as ardently as anyone, in blending an old-fashioned Baptist fervor with a kind of social gospel theology that could transform the black Southern church—making it an instrument, not of docility and other-worldly preoccupations, but a force for earthly change.

Porter added that if I really wanted to understand all that, and how the Kings' double-barreled religious appeal took hold of blacks in the South, I should talk to a retired Birmingham teacher named Claude Wesley. Wesley's connection with the civil rights movement had become painful and intimate on the morning of Sept. 15, 1963. His daughter, Cynthia, was killed in the Birmingham church bombing.

Today, Cynthia's picture hangs above a piano in the Wesley's den. Like many oil portraits, it would have a stately and austere appearance if not for the grin on her round, pretty face. "She was a very happy child," affirmed Wesley, glancing toward the picture. "She always liked to be in the forefront. Her teachers would say that if they could get Cynthia on their side, they could get the whole class."

Wesley smiled and fell silent for a time. He is a slight, almost wispy little man, now 70 and graying. Cynthia was his only child, adopted when she was 6 and killed eight years later. I asked about King's eulogy, about how it feels to be called to such heroic dimensions of Christian forgiveness, when bitterness and rage are more natural inclinations.

Wesley's answer was quick and emphatic. "We never felt bitter," he said. "That wouldn't have been fair to Cynthia. We try to deal with her memory the same way we dealt with her presence, and bitterness has no place in that." He paused to see if I grasped what he was saying, then continued: "There was something else we never did. We never asked, 'Why us?' because that would be the same thing as asking, 'Why not somebody else?'

"But as far as the movement went, we continued to feel about it as we always had. We supported it. We felt it was seeking necessary change, and many changes did come. The '60s emancipated Birmingham. Birmingham is now a good town. It wanted to be a good town then, but it was in the grip of the wrong political hands. But I think everybody knew that the South couldn't stay as it was. Change was going to have to come, and white people make me feel they are just as proud as we are to get rid of this burden."

There is, of course, ample evidence to buttress Claude Wesley's optimism—his view that the South has changed dramatically for the better. Charlotte, N.C. has become a national model for dealing successfully with school desegregation. Alabama and Mississippi have more black elected officials than California. And even Selma, Ala., a symbol of resistance in the 1960s, has made the transition from the politics of race to politics as usual.

Given all that, it is easy to be smug in the South of today. But if you spend a little time in the farmlands of central Alabama (which were, as much as any other place, a focal point for the hatred of King) you find that life goes on pretty much as before. Blacks have been able to solidify some improvements at the polls—electing a sheriff here, a city councilman there—and those things can have tangible effects. But on the economic front, the last frontier proclaimed by King before he was shot in Memphis in 1968, change has been slow at best.

Among the most striking examples of both change and stagnation is Selma. The differences jump out at you first, for in a lot of obvious ways, it's a far more humane and progressive town than in 1965, when the civil rights movement won its last major victory.

Four blacks serve on the city's 11-member council, and black faces are sprinkled throughout city hall. In addition, it's a common conclusion in Selma that the city's white mayor, Joe Smitherman, has abandoned the segregationist policies of his early career—directing millions of federal dollars into improving Selma's black neighborhoods. The reason for the change is simple. Selma's more than 9,000 white voters have been joined by nearly 8,000 blacks, and no politician can ignore either faction.

There's a poetic justice about that reality, for just as Montgomery, and later Birmingham, were pivotal battlegrounds in the fight against legal segregation, Selma was crucial in the battle for the right to vote.

It was a mean and bloody encounter, a final spasm of all-out white resistance to a flow of events that seemed unstoppable. Before the bloodshed ended in the spring of 1965, a white Unitarian minister named James Reeb lay dying in front of a Selma cafe called the Silver Moon—his face beaten beyond recognition and fragments of skull driven into his brain. A few miles east, a Detroit housewife named Viola Liuzzo—one of hundreds of anonymous Northerners on their first trek south in behalf of integration—was gunned down on a winding Alabama backroad.

Such events were a jarring contrast to the tainted tranquility Selma had known. The city hadn't been an oasis, even by black-belt standards, but neither was it a hotbed of black discontent. Two years earlier, when a handful of hardy black organizers (Stokely Carmichael and John Lewis, among others) ventured into town, they were constantly frustrated by the timidity of the people they had come to arouse.

21

"People were scared," remembers Mrs. Theoda Smith, a black, grey-haired Selma native who now runs a day-care center for the city's poor. "We had good reason to be scared, but I remember very well the thing that turned me around. Dr. King and the other organizers had used some children in the picketing and demonstrations. One day my daughter was with a group, and a white man in a car started heading straight for them. He was going to run them down. But this nun, I don't even know her name, had come in from out of town, and she stepped between the car and the kids. The driver didn't want to run over a white lady, a nun at that, so he stopped. Well, I figured then, 'If these people I don't even know can take that kind of risk for my children, it's time for me to do something myself.'"

What Mrs. Smith and the others decided to do was march 50 miles from Selma to Montgomery, demanding voting rights for blacks all over the South. Today, nobody remembers who thought up the idea for a march.

"It just popped up at one of the meetings," says Rev. L. L. Anderson, one of Selma's stalwart black leaders of a decade ago. "It's funny now," adds Anderson, stroking his greying goatee. "If Jim Clark and his men had not been waiting for us at the Edmund Petus Bridge, I don't think we would have made it more than a mile or two down the road. We weren't equipped for a march of that distance. We had no supplies, no arrangements for quarters along the way. All we had was our enthusiasm and our belief that the white leaders would spark a confrontation."

Which, of course, they did.

John Lewis of the Student Non-Violent Coordinating Committee was on the front line, and even today, he says, he has headaches from the beatings he took when mounted, club-wielding deputies swarmed down from the bridge. The press was on hand to record the event, and to transform Jim Clark from a fat and foul-mouthed small-town sheriff into the beady-eyed embodiment of Southern malevolence.

But if Clark overshadowed Selma's other civic leaders, he wasn't the only one in the streets shouting "Never!" nor was he the lone voice of bitter frustration when Martin Luther King flew into town, organized a followup march and secured federal protection from the troops of Lyndon Johnson. Another strident spokesman of the day was Selma's handsome young first-term mayor, Joe Smitherman.

Smitherman was a child of the Alabama Depression—born, like Martin Luther King, in 1929, but coming, unlike King, from a family that was genuinely poor. Today, the mayor takes populist pride in his origins. But in 1965, he concedes, his background had a different effect. It imbued him with the segregationist ardor so common among whites whose economic standing was only a half-step removed from that of most blacks.

22

But there was a key difference between Smitherman and, say, Jim Clark. Clark was voted out of office in an early flexing of black political muscle. Smitherman, on the other hand, learned to cope. He was elected to his fourth term as mayor in 1976, drawing 75 percent of the city's black vote.

Sitting behind his broad-topped wooden desk, flanked on either side by the flags of Alabama and the United States, Smitherman talked freely about changes he has seen. "Like most politicians in Alabama, I was a segregationist," he admits, "and I still have an image among blacks as opposing their movement. But they vote for me today because they don't have any hang-ups about the past, and because they know I'll do what I say.

"You have to give a lot of credit to Martin Luther King. He knew that if, through his non-violence, he could generate a violent response among five percent of the white community, it would sell and the changes would come. But Selma was lucky in a way. The notoriety we received has helped us grow. We got about a billion dollars worth of free advertising, and there's no question that the visibility has helped us in getting federal grants.

"We've used a lot of that money for the benefit of black neighborhoods, which is a good idea for a number of reasons. If you want to improve the quality of this whole town, you take the worst parts of it and work from there. We've had a lot of tangible changes. Our schools have been integrated peacefully. I have two black department heads in my administration, and we have four black city councilmen who have represented their people forcefully.

"I think blacks can look around and see the progress, though economically they have not come nearly as far as they thought they would. As for myself, I find it a lot more comfortable now. It's a relief to be able to talk to a black leader, or a black voter, and not have to look over your shoulder to see who is watching."

It's a revealing spiel, and one that Smitherman delivers nearly every time a visiting journalist wanders into town. But in Selma itself, not everyone is particularly impressed. Over on Jefferson Davis Boulevard, for example, plopped in the middle of a tacky, sun-baked commercial district, are the flat brick law offices of J. L. Chestnut—a Selma native of feisty eloquence, who has emerged in recent years as the city's leading black gadfly.

Almost despite himself, Chestnut takes some wry satisfaction in the altered attitudes of Joe Smitherman. And Chestnut is pleased as well by the sewers and playgrounds, sidewalks and low-cost houses that federal dollars have brought to Selma.

But he argues that for the average black resident of central Alabama, life is far too similar to what is always was. "It's damn near indecent," he says with a sudden oratorical flair, "to talk about how far we've come,

23

until everybody is an American citizen in every sense of the word. That's the mayor's problem. He and I debate each other all the time, and he's one of the most skillful politicians—maybe the most skillful—in the state of Alabama. He's also the primary reason we have not made more progress. Blacks look around and see roads paved, houses owned by people who didn't have them before.

"We don't always understand that it's federal money, and that the feds required it to be spent that way. So we get diverted from the primary issue, which is now economic. It's a complicated question, having to do with how blacks relate to financial institutions, the Small Business Administration, and how much effort employers make to hire blacks in numbers representative of general population. Unless and until we can overcome our complacency enough to mobilize boycotts and other direct action, we are not going to see the changes that are still needed."

Chestnut shifts the subject to the rural Alabama counties where his law firm does a heavy percentage of its practice. There, he points out, the statistics are even more dismal—a median black family income of $2,921, more than 70 percent of the homes without flush toilets, etc. Perhaps the most graphic example of the snail's pace of change, he says, is Lowndes County—a rolling swatch of prairie and timber country a few miles south of Montgomery. It has a black sheriff (a former civil rights leader named John Hulett) and a black superintendent of schools. The county's problem is that economically speaking, there is almost nothing there—no major towns, very few industries, almost no avenues, in short, for life to become less hard.

"This has been a pretty rough place for colored people to live," agreed Harrell Hammonds, as he mopped a shock of white hair from his pale and sweat-streaked forehead. Hammonds is Lowndes County's probate judge, a craggy-faced, life-long resident who has amassed, over the years, some 20,000 acres of land and a remarkable reputation for noblesse oblige decency.

Even in the 1950s, Hammonds argued that blacks and whites should be treated equally in court. Later, he would support black representation on the Lowndes County Board of Education, and a black superintendent of schools. For all of that, he paid a price. His house burned under mysterious circumstances, and threats on his life became almost commonplace.

But Hammonds isn't a man of self-pity, and when he talks of the violence of the past, he focuses not on the anxiety he felt himself, but on the larger, more hideous tragedies—the capricious, commonplace beatings of blacks in the night, and the fatal shooting, in 1965, of a white civil rights worker named Jonathan Daniels.

Hammonds believes that when Daniels, a soft-spoken Episcopal priest, stepped out of the Lowndes County Store with a moon pie and a Pepsi, only to have a load of buckshot slam into his chest from point-blank range, it was an event condoned by most white people in the area. Everybody knew that Daniels was a believer in the dream of Martin Luther King, that he was a New England radical whose sole motivation for coming to Alabama was to tear at the state's way of life. The man who never denied pulling the trigger, Thomas Coleman, became a local hero and a district supervisor for the state Department of Engineers.

But those days are passing now, and for Hammonds it's a source of considerable relief. "I think a lot of people feel that same way," he adds. "Even in the bad times, there were people who wanted to do what was right, but they were afraid, or they didn't know where to start. I think most people will tell you the changes had to come. They were long overdue."

But primarily, of course, they were changes in the life of Harrell Hammonds. No longer was he faced with the possibility of violent reprisals, and even more importantly perhaps, he could finally feel some pride, rather than shame, in the attitudes around him. In the end, the angle of vision is crucial, and the final irony may be that the world has changed more for whites in the South than it has for blacks.

Earvin Hinson, at least, believes that's the case. Hinson, like Judge Hammonds, comes from a family that has lived in Lowndes County since before the Civil War. But instead of owning 20,000 acres, he owns 100—a rough, briar-infested piece of turf where almost nothing grows.

Hinson is a black man—a burly, 42-year-old truck-driving farmer that I met by accident. I was driving down a random dirt road in central Lowndes County when it ended abruptly in a gravel-covered clearing a few feet from Hinson's farmhouse. He hadn't been at home when I started down the road, but came speeding up in his truck—arriving in a cloud of dust only a few seconds after I stopped.

He stepped between me and the half dozen children who stared from his porch, and waited with a quiet, almost friendly defiance. I explained what I wanted, and after a stare that said, "I'm not really sure I believe you but on the other hand I don't really care," he leaned against the sagging farmhouse steps and began a soliloquy on how things have been.

"Rough," he said. "A few years back, I was driving home one night, and my car broke down. It was late and while I was sitting there trying to decide what to do, these white guys came up and gave me a hell of a head-whippin'. They tied my hands behind my back and stuffed me in the trunk of a car. They must have driven around for hours, and when they stopped, my shirt and everything else was covered with blood.

"About dawn, this highway patrolman came up and tried to yank me out of the trunk by my belt. I wouldn't let him—I had my feet braced against the side—and finally he said, 'Nigger get out of that trunk.' I did, and after a while they let me go."

Hinson settled himself in a flimsy metal chair, then continued: "It's a little better today than it was. We have a black man for sheriff now, so you don't have to worry so much about the head-whippin's. But a lot of things are still the same. I ain't got any running water on this place. The white man who owns the place next door, he's got running water. You know why? 'Cause white people want this land.

"Yeah," he concluded with an anger that seemed almost matter-of-fact, "It's better than it has been, but it ain't justice."

Leaving Lowndes County with the words of Earvin Hinson still rumbling in my head, I passed an enormous road sign just east of Montgomery. The sign affirmed in big block letters that Alabama's lawmakers had renamed the road the Martin Luther King Memorial Expressway.

It offered a juxtaposition that was somehow depressing between the official sanctification of King and the unfinished business of his movement. I began to think about the opening scene of Abby Mann's movie, an unsettling piece of footage to King's less critical admirers.

It's the vision of a man about to be snatched into martyrdom from the edge of defeat—of a stunned and bewildered Martin Luther King, caught in the middle of a Memphis mob. The people of the mob are black—bitter and taunting; contemptuous, it seems, to the point of hatred for King and his Baptist non-violence.

Nobody knows, of course, what would have happened if the bullet had missed in Memphis and King had lived. But this much is clear. If the man was martyred, the movement was not. In the end, it simply faded away, leaving the masses of black people (those outside the American middle class) almost as far from the promised land as they ever were before.

But perhaps the final, dollars-in-the-pocket success is beyond the power of one man's eloquence; for no matter how much the followers of King would have us focus on all that remains to be done, it's impossible to have lived in the South for the past 20 years and to remain unawed by the things that have happened—the enfranchisement of one race of people, and the redemption, grudging to be sure, of the hearts and minds of another.

Back at the swimming pool of the Macon Hilton, Yolanda King talked about the improbability of it all—of a young and uncertain preacher inspired by the fatigue and dignity of a woman on a bus.

As she spoke, she let her eyes wander out across the people at the pool—Hollywood people, with their Polaroid glasses and chic, clingy bathing suits. The faint suggestion of a frown settled on her brow, and it seemed, at least, as if the multiple incongruities of the setting had their effect. "People are so cynical today," she said, with soft and unabashed sentimentality. "But I think Daddy was a God-sent man. It's hard to explain it any other way."

CHAPTER 2

The Black Emergence:
1945-65

Early in 1982, the Charlotte Observer undertook a Black History Month series on the saga of race relations in North Carolina and South Carolina. My assignment was to cover two decades, from 1945 to 1965, a time of ferment and an eventual sense of progress—a sort of We-Shall-Overcome momentum beginning near the end of World War II and continuing until the passage of the Voting Rights Act.

During that period—amid the sit-ins, marches and precedent-breaking lawsuits—blacks in the Carolinas and elsewhere were united in an assault on legal segregation. Jim Crow laws were abundant. North Carolina and South Carolina required segregated washrooms in factories and cotton mills, and both states were among 17 that segregated their schools.

In the next 15 years, a great deal would change. Dual public schools were ordered dismantled. Congress passed laws against segregated public accommodations, and after a bloodstained march from Selma to Montgomery, blacks secured sweeping protections under the Voting Rights Act. Those titanic changes often began in the simplest of ways—with four frustrated freshmen in a dormitory bull session, or with a handful of farmers, country preachers and gas station attendants who wanted nothing more than a bus for their school children.

Here, in those human terms, is a history of the period, beginning with the events in rural South Carolina that led, in the late 1940s, to the first successful challenge to segregated schools.

February, 1982

Part 1: The Schools

They began coming home from the South Pacific jungles, from Okinawa, Iwo Jima and the seas in between. Harry Briggs was one of them. He left the Navy after the surrender of Japan and returned to Summerton, S.C., where he had lived all his life.

Briggs, a solid, slightly round-faced man in his early thirties, was the father of five, a reliable provider who made his living pumping Sinclair gas at Carrigan's Service Station. He borrowed a little money from his preacher-friend, J. A. DeLaine, and built himself a house near Scott's Branch School.

Like other black people in Clarendon County, he was not especially impressed with the quality of the schools. He didn't know the statistics—how the whites who ran the public education system in that majority-black county spent $179 a year on each white student and $43 a year on each black.

But he didn't have to know statistics to know that life was unfair in Clarendon County, a flat and tangled collection of hardwood forests and loamy cotton fields about half way between Columbia and Charleston.

Political and economic power was in the hands of whites, and fewer than 300 of Clarendon's 4,600 black households earned as much as $2,000 a year. Harry Briggs understood the realities behind such figures, and like any rational man, he did not expect them to change.

Still, he had fought for his country during World War II. He had risked his life to defend American freedom, and it seemed that he and his people deserved something for that.

Like a school bus, perhaps.

In 1947, blacks in Clarendon County had petitioned for one—particularly to serve a small group of children near the community of Jordan, who had to walk nine miles around a lake, or else row a boat across it, to get to school.

But R.W. Elliott, a white sawmill owner and chairman of the school board, told the blacks simply: "We ain't got no money to buy a bus for your nigger children."

Harry Briggs didn't think that was fair. Nor did he approve when the chief petitioner for the bus, a fiftyish farmer named Levi Pearson, was denied credit by all of Clarendon's banks, nor when Elliott's sawmill refused to haul the timber that Pearson had cut to pay his bills, leaving it instead to rot on the ground.

So Briggs decided to fight back. He was not the leader in the fight; that task fell to J. A. DeLaine, the local spokesman for the NAACP. But Briggs did offer his house for strategy sessions, and alphabetically he became the first of 20 plaintiffs in the lawsuit of Briggs v. Elliott.

It was no ordinary lawsuit. Initially, it demanded equal schools for the black and white children of Clarendon County. But eventually, under the prodding of the NAACP's chief attorney, Thurgood Marshall, Harry Briggs and the other Clarendon blacks demanded a national dismantling of segregated schools—a move eventually affecting more than 11.5 million students in 17 states.

They paid a price for that demand. On Christmas Eve of 1949, Briggs was fired from his job at Carrigan's Service Station, and his wife, Liza, shortly lost her maid's job at a Summerton motel.

For J. A. DeLaine, the reprisals were worse. He was dismissed from his principal's position at a Clarendon County school and driven from his home by late-night gunfire. But Briggs and DeLaine would not relent, and their courage was supported by the thoroughness of the NAACP's legal staff and by the sympathetic ear of a federal district judge.

The judge was a patrician from Charleston, S.C. His name was J. Waties Waring, and he lived at 61 Meeting St. in a house that dated to the 17th century, nestled among the palms and wisteria and the stands of live oaks near the Charleston harbor.

Waring was a quiet man with sharply pointed features, his hair parted down the middle with aristocratic precision. He was 61 years old when he ascended to the federal bench, and from the beginning he had taken deep offense at civil rights violations.

Thurgood Marshall was aware of Waring's reputation. He was comforted by it, for the stakes were high and risky in Briggs vs. Elliott. Marshall knew that if he lost—if the courts affirmed the legality of segregation, as they had done at the turn of the century—the cause of black people would be set back irreparably.

Painstakingly, he constructed his case—first by documenting the inferiority of Clarendon County's black schools. Then, in a tactic that would later prove crucial, he set out to demonstrate the effects of segregation on the self-esteem of children.

Marshall asked for help from Dr. Kenneth Clark, a 37-year-old psychiatrist from City College of New York, who visited Clarendon County in 1951. Using a box full of black and white dolls, Clark conducted a series of experiments.

He asked 16 black children between the ages of 6 and 9 which dolls they liked best. According to Richard Kluger, whose book *Simple Justice* is the definitive history of the period, 10 children preferred the white dolls; 11 said the black dolls looked "bad."

In 1954, when Chief Justice Earl Warren wrote the Supreme Court's historic ruling, affirming Judge Waring's opinion that official segregation was unconstitutional, he was deeply moved by the tests Clark had conducted. They buttressed a feeling that he had, a simple gut certainty that segregated schools were damaging to children and inevitably unequal.

So, writing for the court, Warren declared them illegal.

The ruling applied to Clarendon County and to four other places where dual schools had been challenged—Prince Edward County, Va., Wilmington, Del., Washington, D.C. and Topeka, Kan. In addition, the precedent affected 11,168 other school districts that practiced official segregation. It was, morally and legally, the greatest victory that blacks had ever achieved.

The problem was that nothing much came of it.

In Clarendon County, the schools quickly became all-black, as white

1957: Dorothy Counts Approaches Charlotte's
Harding High School

parents—every single one of them before it was over—sent their children to private schools, rather than permit integration.

And throughout the South, most whites seemed embarked on a path of massive resistance. In 1957, for example, when Elizabeth Eckford and eight other black teenagers integrated Central High School in Little Rock, Ark., federal troops were required to protect them from the mobs.

The same year in Charlotte, a theology professor's daughter named Dorothy Counts—dressed in a prim checkered dress with a white bow at the collar—endured jeers and taunts as she enrolled in Harding High School. Two weeks later, she dropped out, after being spat upon regularly and pelted with rocks.

Most cities, meanwhile, simply ignored the Supreme Court's ruling, and segregation remained a reality in the South. So blacks grew impatient. They began to challenge Jim Crow laws and customs more directly than before: they simply refused to obey them.

In 1960, for example, four black college students demanded to be served at an all-white lunch counter. It was the first sit-in, and after it happened on that wintry day in Greensboro, N.C., the civil rights struggle gained a momentum it had never known.

This is how it came to be.

Part 2: The Protests

It was cold that night. Too cold, they decided, to go anywhere. So they settled in about 7 and began to talk and play chess. After a while, they could feel an all-nighter coming on.

They had had such sessions before—right there, in fact, in room 2123 with its drab green walls and off-white ceilings, the clutter of magazines scattered on the floor.

The room belonged to Joe McNeil and Ezell Blair. McNeil was studying physics, and the latest Physics Today had been tossed on the pile amid the old Atlantic Monthlys. There were philosophy texts and assorted paperbacks by Eric Hoffer and Nikos Kazantzakis.

But the talk that evening, Jan. 31, 1960, seldom strayed to classwork. McNeil, Blair and their two friends from down the hall, Franklin McCain and David Richmond, were caught up once again in the central reality of their lives.

They were black students at N.C. A&T, a state university in Greensboro, N.C. All were freshmen—scholarship students from middle-class families—and from the beginning, they had sensed a philosophical affinity.

They would talk about the conditions afflicting their people, the insulting Jim Crow laws that had sprung up around the South at the turn of the century. They would rail at the patience of their parents' genera-

Franklin McCain, 1980

tion—people who had fought a world war to preserve American freedom, but who had failed to find a way to demand it for themselves.

The next day, these young men would make such a demand. They would make it in a way that commanded national attention, that generated a sense of movement and momentum for blacks across the South, and that tied in with earlier stirrings in Montgomery, Ala.—a bus boycott led by a then-obscure preacher named Martin Luther King.

Joe McNeil and the others were aware of that boycott. They approved of it, but gave it little thought, for it seemed to them an isolated event. They were aware also of the legal strides in the field of education, the historic 1954 Supreme Court decision on segregated schools.

But what they felt most keenly was a sense of stagnation, at best of fits and starts, in the progress of their people. They had analyzed the subject from every conceivable angle—from the philosophical theories of Immanuel Kant and G. W. F. Hegel, to the social commentary of W. E. B. DuBois.

But as they noted that night, they themselves had done nothing. McNeil, more than any of them, kept pointing that out. He was the boat-rocker, the bright, impatient son of a cleaning company operator in Wilmington, N.C.

Blair and Richmond, both from Greensboro, were the steadiest of the group, and they insisted at least on a reasonable course of action, a carefully conceived plan, if they were to challenge the social order. McCain, a chemistry major from Washington, D.C., tended to share McNeil's impatience, and he remembers the dynamics of the discussion that evening:

"The question kept re-emerging," he says. " 'What are we going to do? Will we leave here as seniors still just debating? We can't sit back and wait. We've done nothing but engage in armchair rhetoric. We ought to feel badly about ourselves. It makes us less than men.' "

They began to talk about public accommodations—how nearby stores like Walgreen's and Woolworth's would accept their money happily, but refused to serve them at their greasy spoon lunch counters.

"We said to ourselves," remembers McCain, " 'If we tolerate it, to an extent, we probably deserve it.' "

Shortly after 5 a.m. on Feb. 1, their bodies aching and eyes gazing blearily at the grayish streaks of dawn, they decided to "sit in"—a term that would soon become popular among blacks across the South—at a nearby lunch counter.

They thought of Walgreen's but chose Woolworth's instead because it was a much larger chain with stores across the country. They agreed to meet at the campus library at 4 that afternoon.

McCain remembers being distracted that day. He made it through chemistry and geometry and a discussion of James Thurber in English Composition. But he picked up several demerits in ROTC, his last class of the day, for speaking without permission.

Finally, at 3:30, he headed for the library where he met the other three. At 4, having given up on a handful of friends who promised reinforcements, they started off on the 10-minute walk to Woolworth's.

They arrived at the store and began meandering among the aisles, buying school supplies and keeping the receipts. As it happened, McCain and McNeil were closest to the lunch counter, and McCain recalls the strange mix of feelings:

"Apprehension. Anxiety. A fear of the unknown. I can't define explicitly what I had anxiety about, except that it's hard to plan an adequate defense if you don't know what will happen.

"So we just looked at that counter. We stood there maybe a minute, maybe five. Then McNeil and I looked at each other, looked at the counter again and then stepped toward it.

"The moment we sat down at that counter . . . well, I just can't tell you what it felt like. Never have I experienced such an incredible emotion, such an uplift in my life. My good friend from Atlanta, (journalist) Howell Raines, probably said it best: 'My soul was rested.'

"Everything else that ever happens is probably downhill from that. I don't think it's possible for me to crystallize that feeling, and in most conversations I don't even try—because the words are not adequate, because they can sound very foolish and pretentious."

In any case, says McCain, they took their seats on the padded swivel stools, beneath the signs for 10-cent coffee and 15-cent lemon pie—McCain still in his ROTC uniform, with his black-rimmed glasses and small, thin mustache; McNeil more boyish and slightly sad-faced—waiting for the waitress to come and tell them to leave.

She did come and tell them, a slightly flustered white woman, brown-haired and average-sized, maybe 40 years old with the look of middle age. She said, "We don't serve Negroes here."

That had happened before at Woolworth's. What was new was the resistance—McCain speaking softly with a manicured politeness: "I beg to disagree. You do serve us and you have." And McNeil added stubbornly: "We have the receipts to prove it."

A policeman arrived about that time and began to pace near the scene, tapping his nightstick firmly in his palm. The waitress, meanwhile, went to fetch the manager, James Harris, as Blair and Richmond, who had been across the store, arrived to take their seats at the counter near McCain.

The tension grew.

"I just can't serve you," said Harris, obviously the man in charge, with his blue suit, white shirt and carefully knotted tie.

Why? he was asked.

"Because it's custom," said Harris, his frustration mounting, but also a pained confusion, a collision between his decency and the logic of the argument that now confronted him. Still, he would not relent:

"There's a counter downstairs. It's custom. You can get anything you want."

The crowd began to grow as word spread of the stand-off. Maybe 200 whites were watching near the counter, their mood a mixture of curiosity and resentment. More were gathering on the sidewalk outside, staring in through the windows that faced Elm Street.

Harris left and the crowd still glared. But one of their number, an aging white woman with a feisty air about her, approached the four young men still sitting at the counter. She patted their backs, and told them loudly enough for anyone to overhear:

"Boys, I'm so proud of you. The only thing is, it should have been done 20 years ago."

That was the high point. The low point came when a black kitchen worker berated the four for their impatience and presumption. "Why don't you just get up and leave," she pleaded with them finally.

"At that moment," says McCain, now an executive with Celanese Corp. in Charlotte, N.C., "we literally hated her. Later, I felt differently. I came to understand how we threatened her world and the order she was used to. She could see no good coming out of what we were doing."

The good came, however.

The four left that day when James Harris closed the store. But they returned the next morning with maybe 20 of their friends, and by that afternoon, every stool at the counter was occupied by blacks.

The national press arrived. Woolworth's eventually gave in, and the sit-in tactic spread across the South, as blacks of varied backgrounds—middle-class and poor—took common offense at official segregation.

Their primary spokesman, in the eyes of the national press, and increasingly in the eyes of Southern blacks as well, became Martin Luther King, an eloquent preacher of some reluctance, who, at the least, had been trained for his role.

Some of the training came from his father, Martin Luther King, Sr., an Atlanta preacher who dreamed of revitalizing the Southern black church, making it a force for social change.

The younger King's other mentor was a South Carolinian named Benjamin Mays, a sharecropper's son, born in Greenwood County at the pinnacle of Reconstruction, when the presumed inferiority of his people became a matter of law—of official policy in his home-state and elsewhere.

"I never did accept what my eyes saw and what my ears heard," says

Mays, now in his late eighties and living in Atlanta. "Everything around me said to me that I and my people were inferior. Negroes were constantly cringing and kowtowing in the presence of white people.

"I remember when I was 4 years old, a mob of whites came by my father's house. They were on their way to the town of Phoenix, where a black man had tried to register to vote.

"But they stopped and made my father take off his hat, bow down and salute. They were armed, and they made him scrape and humble himself. I didn't think that was right."

The episode, which offended a 4-year-old's sense of fairness, stayed with Mays as he made his way through school, then to S.C. State College in Orangeburg, Virginia Union, predominantly white Bates College in Maine, and finally to his doctorate in theology from the University of Chicago.

As the honors piled atop each other, Mays began to absorb not only the learning itself, but a lesson so fundamental that it became an obsession: "I was trying to demonstrate," he says, "that I was not inferior. "

Eventually, he believed it and set out to teach other blacks as well. He became president of Atlanta's Morehouse College, and one of his most willing students, in the years following World War II, was Martin Luther King, Jr.

Mays thought the religion he experienced as a child in South Carolina was a barrier as well as a solace to blacks. He wrote:

"I heard the pastor of the church of my youth plead with members of his congregation not to try to avenge the wrongs they suffered, but to take their burdens to the Lord in prayer. Especially did he do this when the racial situation was tense or when Negroes went to him for advice concerning some wrong inflicted upon them by their oppressors." The pastor assured them "that God would fix things up" and "would reward them in heaven for their patience and long suffering on the earth.

"Members of the congregation screamed, shouted and thanked God. They felt relieved and uplifted. . . . They sang, prayed and shouted their troubles away. This had telling effects on the Negroes in my home community. It kept them submissive, humble and obedient. It enabled them to keep on keeping on."

Like the elder King, Mays believed in the potential of the Southern black church; it was, after all, the only institution that blacks had been allowed. And he brought black scholars to Morehouse College, who instructed the students in the tactical non-violence of Mahatma Ghandi.

In 1956, the younger King was able to put his training to use. The opportunity, however, took him by surprise, for unlike the four students in Greensboro, his friend Rosa Parks had given it no advance

Benjamin Mays, 1978

thought when she refused, on a Montgomery bus, to relinquish her seat to a white man who demanded it. She was simply tired.

And after she was arrested and taken off to jail, Montgomery's black community was almost universally insulted—shocked that a woman like Mrs. Parks, a respected teacher with an air of great dignity, could be treated so shabbily.

They rallied to her defense by boycotting the buses, and they chose King as their spokesman. He was a good choice. He was only 26 and completely untested by the trials of leadership. But already he had a gift that would continue to develop over the next 12 years—an oratorical flair that was probably unsurpassed by any man of his century.

Partly it was a simple question of pulpit showmanship, the sense of cadence and momentum, the dramatic rise and fall of his voice. But more than that, he had a certain perspective, an ability to reassure his people through all the victories and tragedies that made up the movement—the church bombings in Birmingham, the murdered civil rights workers in Alabama and Mississippi —that "the arc of the moral universe is long, but it bends toward justice."

He told them such things in Washington in 1963, on a late summer's day when 170,000 black people and their white allies marched peacefully on the capital. There were only three arrests that day—two thugs and a Nazi—as King proclaimed improbable thoughts and dreams about the future of the South:

"I have a dream today . . . that one day on the red hills of Georgia, the sons of former slaves and the sons of former slaveowners will be able to sit down together at the table of brotherhood."

For a while, it almost seemed possible. Congress passed a strong civil rights bill in 1964, outlawing segregation in public accommodations.

Then, in 1965, King led his most important march—a trek from Selma to Montgomery, an occasion in which one of his followers, James Reeb, was beaten to death outside a Selma cafe, and another, Viola Liuzzo, was killed by gunfire on an Alabama backroad.

Congress responded by passing the Voting Rights Act, assuring blacks in the South of access to the ballot. The result over the next 15 years was a stunning increase in the number of black elected officials—from fewer than two dozen in the Carolinas to 485 in 1980.

Things, however, began to sour after that. The summers exploded, as blacks rioted regularly in major cities around the country, burning the neighborhoods in which they felt themselves trapped. For even though they could vote or eat where they chose, millions of them experienced little improvement in their lives.

They were as poor, and felt as victimized, as they ever had before. And that feeling was at the heart of an uncertainty, a dilemma and a division, that began to afflict the black movement.

Until the Voting Rights Act and the other gains of the '60s, blacks were united by a common reality: the shared insult of official segregation.

But that bond was broken—ironically enough, by the progress of the movement—and blacks found themselves in a subtle new period. The challenge was now economic, and some of them met it nicely: During the 1960s, black family income increased by 141 percent in North Carolina and nearly 162 percent in South Carolina.

But millions of blacks remained desperately poor—and no longer, it seemed, were their interests indistinguishable from those of the middle class. Ralph Abernathy, who took over Martin Luther King's organization after King was murdered in 1968, offered this summary of the new dilemmas of leadership:

"It's a difficult period," he said in frustration. "Very hard to get a handle on exactly what to do."

CHAPTER 3

The Scandalous Gospel
of Will Campbell

One of the most influential, and intermittently famous, of the South's white Chris-
tian disciples and civil rights advocates is Will Campbell, a Baptist renegade now liv-
ing in Nashville. His career began in Mississippi with his support of integration in
the 1950s, and it took him to most of the civil rights trouble spots in the 1960s. But
Campbell's radical Christian visions also led him to the other side of the street, to
friendships with members of the Ku Klux Klan. More recently, he has spoken out
against capital punishment and abortion, and all of it is rooted in his understanding
of the faith—which is, it's safe to say, distinctly his own.

January, 1981

I stopped off in Nashville a short while back for a few days of R & R
with my friend, Will Campbell, a balding, funny-looking, hard-living
preacher—a Baptist-bred drinking buddy and spiritual advisor who has
emerged over the years as a Socratic Southern gadfly, a thorn in the
flesh of the conventional wisdom. I arrived a little late for the christen-
ing—the spiritual dedication of the newborn son of Waylon Jennings
(an event attended by, among others, Muhammad Ali). But I did catch
a glimpse of the burial of Bill Jenkins, which was in itself a remarkable
occasion. Jenkins was a neighbor of Campbell's—an 85-year-old black
man who lived alone and who would peer from his farmhouse porch
across the rolling Tennessee countryside, recalling the days when it all
belonged to him, before the depression came and the banks foreclosed
and his children grew up and moved away. "The younger generation,"
he would say, "they so crazy. Always causin' trouble 'bout this or that.
Me," he would say, "I ain't ever been in no trouble . . ." then adding for
the sake of clinical accuracy after gazing discreetly at the curling,
light-skinned scar that ran across his wrist and left thumb, " 'cept when
I killed my wife."

But all that was a long time ago, and Jenkins had long since done his
time and paid his debts and lived hard and clean for more than 50
years. Then he died, and as the mourners poured into the sandstone

church, making their way across a rubble-strewn field of briars and Johnson grass and Queen Anne's lace, Campbell stood before them, grimly buoyed by the swelling amens and the grief-stricken moans, and he declared in sonorous tones: "He was my neighbor. We used to lean against the fence and swap stories in the evenin' time, but that wasn't enough. No it wasn't enough because he was also my friend. It didn't matter that he was old, and I was not so old, or that his skin was black and mine was white, or that he owned a lot of land and I owned a little. He was my friend. But that wasn't enough either 'cause he was also my brother . . ."

And later, when a friend with no connection to the event beyond curiosity offered lame compliments on the quality of the sermon, Campbell simply grunted and cleared his throat. "Hell," he affirmed, his boot kicking idly at the Tennessee sod, "if you can't preach to a bunch of broken-hearted people, there ain't much use in trying to preach. . . ."

Campbell can preach, of course. He's been at it now for more than 40 years, ever since the steamy June Sunday in south Mississippi, when he preached his first sermon at East Fork Baptist, a tiny wooden church near the town of Liberty—hidden away in the murky Amite County bottomlands, amid the stands of pine and the shadowy streams of gray Spanish moss. He gazed out nervously across the upturned faces—a skinny, soft-eyed kid of 17, with oversized ears and a runaway shock of dark brown hair. He peered through a pair of black-rimmed glasses, and after checking the hand-me-down pocket watch on the lectern beside him, he launched a short, fiery sermon on the first verse of Genesis.

Later, after thinking it over and praying about it some, the elders of the church—preacher J. Price Brock and a half dozen others—took him aside and declared him ordained to go and preach the gospel. He made a few detours along the way, through Yale Divinity School, among other places, but he has emerged in the end as one of the South's leading preachers—an earthy, erudite theologian and author who takes satisfaction in giving offense, in proclaiming a kind of scandalous, radicalized vision of the faith, producing shock and astonishment nearly anywhere he goes.

He is not a William Sloane Coffin. Nor is he Billy Graham. He is instead an odd and unsettling combination of the two—a radical, slow-moving Bible-belt preacher with a hand-carved cane and a floppy Amish hat, meandering his way through the crises of life. He's developed a kind of cult-figure fame in American theology, partly through his books, but mostly through his unpretentious, one-man ministry to the nation's dispossessed. He's an ardent proponent of

black civil rights, a friend to the bigots in the Ku Klux Klan, and most recently, an unlikely champion for the men and women of death row.

He began in the '50s with the issue of race. First as chaplain at the University of Mississippi, and later as a Deep South staffer for the National Council of Churches, he allied himself with the civil rights movement—traveling the bumpy Southern backroads from one upheaval to the next, from Montgomery to Nashville to St. Augustine, Fla.

It's hard to say exactly what he did. He was simply there, moving among the people and offering what he could. In 1957, for example, he was one of three white ministers with Elizabeth Eckford, walking by her side as she and eight other black teenagers made their way through the Little Rock mobs, braving taunts and rocks and bayonetted rifles, seeking to enroll in an all-white school.

Gradually, he became a friend to the leaders of the movement—Andy Young, John Lewis and Martin Luther King—but also to the bright young radicals of lesser charisma, some of them filled with foolhardy courage, others simply quiet and determined, as they drifted into Selma or Marks, Miss., defying the wrath of the most brutal South. Campbell was awed by the bravery of it all, and yet he couldn't shake a feeling in the back of his mind—a troublesome sense that however right and righteous it was, however important that the South be confronted with the sins of its history, there was something simplistic and shortsighted about the whole crusade, some failure to understand, as he would put it later, "that Mr. Jesus died for the bigots as well."

So he began to work the other side of the street, mingling with the racists and Klansmen, as well as the blacks, setting out from home in the early morning hours, rumbling through the Delta in his cherry-red pick-up. Armed with a guitar and a Bible and an occasional bottle of Tennessee whiskey, he would point himself toward the flat and muddy fields of Sunflower County, toward the straight and endless rows of picked-over cotton and the barbed-wire fences of Parchman Penitentiary.

At Parchman, he would visit a young friend of his—a terrorist, as it happened, whose name was Tommy Tarrants. He was a Klansman, a tough and lanky young man in his middle twenties, with scruffy brown hair and a head full of hate. He had moved to Mississippi from Mobile, Ala., becoming, while he was still in his teens, a leading strategist in a campaign of violence. But he was shot and nearly killed in 1968, ambushed by the FBI, as he sought to bomb the home of a liberal Jewish merchant. For his trouble, he was sentenced to 30 years in prison, and at the time Campbell came along, he was still in a struggle with the passions of his youth.

They spent a lot of time behind the barbed wire of Parchman, settling occasionally under the shade of an oak and letting the conversation ramble where it would. Eventually, after visits from Campbell and a handful of others who took an interest in his case, Tarrants began to change. He renounced his racism, proclaimed a newfound belief in the Christian faith, and got himself paroled. He enrolled in Ole Miss, got a degree, and became a kind of free-lance missionary to the prisoners of the South.

Campbell is pleased by that, but takes no credit for it. Conversions, he says, are not his calling. He is embarked instead on an unconditional ministry, a simple reaching out to angry young blacks, Kluxers, draft-dodgers and alienated rich—leaving it to them what they do with the message. That's a little unsettling to many fundamentalists, and also to his liberal friends, to the people who are involved in a push for social change. But for Campbell, it's all very clear, and he will rummage through the clutter on his rolltop desk, producing a well-worn copy of the King James Bible, fumbling through the parchment to the writings of Paul.

"Here," he will say, "it's all right here in Second Corinthians, right down here at the end of chapter five: 'God was in Christ, reconciling the world unto himself, not imputing their trespasses against them. . . .'

"There," he continues, with a fierce, sudden swipe at his gray fringe of hair, "that's what it's all about. You can read it there, or in Mark or Matthew, or over in Luke. But what it all means is so damn simple: we are bastards, but God loves us anyway. We're forgiven, and if we can somehow manage to get hold of that fact, we can find the power to go and do likewise. Go and hate no more, go and kill no more. Old Tommy Tarrants got his mind around that one, and if the rest of us could do the same . . . but of course we don't want to do the same 'cause it would change the way we all do our business. So we keep foolin' around with all the false messiahs . . ." and he shrugs philosophically, folds up the Bible and returns it roughly to the clutter on his desk.

But despite his fatalism and occasional despair, Campbell has set out to proclaim the message—giving little thought to measurable results, for if he did much of that, he would give up the ghost. He is a peculiar sort of gospel existentialist, like some strange character from the mind of Camus, behaving as if the odds were not insurmountable—as if the world were not full of murder, mendacity, executions and prejudice.

It is, he admits, a mission so pure and pitiful that it's almost a joke. But it *isn't* a joke, for not everyone is amused when he pays a visit to a rich liberal church, surveying the stained glass windows and the prosperous people in the hand-carved pews—and suggesting, when they ask how their faith should be applied, that they leave the door to the sanctuary open, so the downtown winos will have a place to sleep.

"I agree," he says, "that they'll use bad language, and maybe piss on your rug. But it's scriptural."

And if that sounds outrageous to the point of buffoonery, there are other moments when he can't be dismissed, when the scandal of his message is so inescapable that the people in the audience will wince, or even cry, as the words tumble out. He is strangely unimposing as he stands before them, looking thoroughly uncomfortable, tugging at his earlobe or the end of his sideburn, ignoring, or trying to, the knot of fear and insecurity that is there in his gut. There is the trace of a tremor around the edges of his voice, and yet through it all a kind of resonant, stentorian certainty as he begins to tell the story.

It is a brutal story and the telling is as wrenching as Campbell can make it.

"Thirty-four years ago," he says, speaking this time to more than 12,000 teenagers, Lutherans as it happens, who are gathered in Kansas City for their annual convention, "I stood with my buddies on the island of Saipan, overlooking the crystal blue waters of the Pacific Ocean. Not far from where we stood was a little island, looking to us almost like an aircraft carrier—a little island called Tinian. We used to stand in the early morning and watch the big airplanes take off and gather in the afternoon to watch them return. That day, Aug. 6, 1945 . . . was no ordinary day. It was the day 200,000 human beings would die. It was the day the first atom bomb was dropped. . . .

"We knew as we gathered that afternoon that the bomb had fallen, 200,000 people left dead in its wake . . . and I cheered! My young brothers and sisters, I yelled and cheered and slapped my buddies on the back and threw my Army helmet into the sea at the news that 200,000 people, those for whom Christ died, no longer lived. Because I wanted to go home. Fry the bastards. Kill the slant-eyed, slope-head sons-of-bitches. I want to go home. . . ."

He pauses now to let the words sink in, his expression a mixture of outrage and grief, eyes glistening, his hand trembling slightly at the side of the lectern. But his words are soft and sure as he resumes the narrative, shifting the scene to another cheering crowd of more recent vintage—to the people who gathered May 25, 1979, to applaud the excruciating end to the life of John Spenkelink. Shortly after 10:00 on that sunny May morning, amid the taunting of guards and the jubilant chanting of the people outside, Spenkelink was strapped to a white wooden chair at the Florida state prison. And on the final orders of Gov. Bob Graham, 7,500 volts of electricity were sent through his body, causing his flesh to burn, and six minutes later, his heart to stop beating.

In the aftermath of that execution, Campbell has emerged as one of the nation's leading opponents of capital punishment—denouncing it, testifying against it wherever he can. For he knew John Spenkelink's history, knew that he was guilty of killing another man, but also that in his nearly six years of facing death himself, he had become caught up in a quiet Christian search, not showy or pious, but a final private grappling with what it all means. He was the acknowledged leader among the men of death row—aggressive in defense of other prisoners' rights, but with an emerging sensitivity that was sometimes startling. Two hours before his death, for example, he turned to his minister and friend, Tom Feamster, and said, "Let's pray for the governor . . ." adding when the prayer was over, "Don't tell the press. That's not why I did it. . . ."

Campbell told all that to his young Lutheran audience, then compared it starkly to the things that happened next.

"When all was in readiness," he said, his voice low and husky, but strangely calm, "when Brother John, bound and gagged, was strapped in the electric chair, the curtain was opened for the witnesses. The first surge, 2,500 volts of electricity, singed the skin off his right calf, sending smoke into the death chamber. He clenched his left fist, then his hands began to curl and blacken. Listen to me now. The doctor stepped forth, unbuttoned his white shirt and placed a stethoscope on his chest. He was not yet dead. The doctor stepped back. Another surge of 2,500 volts of electricity, then another, and the deed was done. And outside the walls, a group of teenage hecklers about your age, 15, 16, 19 years, were chanting in unison, again and again: 'Spark Spenk, Spark Spenk, Bring On The Barbecue Sauce.' I wanted to cry, to run, to vomit. And I did cry, for I was hearing myself, 34 years ago, cheering on the cliffs of a faraway island . . . 'Fry the bastards, kill the sons-of-bitches. I want to go home. . . .' "

And there in the auditorium filled with silence and shock, just before the outburst of a standing ovation, Campbell added six words—sounding at first like an afterthought, but making, he says, the only real point that he knows how to make: "May Christ have mercy upon us."

That is his hope, his pitch, his final affirmation when it all gets crazy. Though his thinking is systematic in its own peculiar way, it is more than an abstraction from St. Augustine or Paul, more than an echo of his professors back at Yale. There's a kind of brutal intuition about reality and religion, a sure wrathful instinct that keeps him on course. But where does it come from? What is it, finally, that saves him from despair, yet removes him as well from the pristine and pious?

To get a sense of that, it helps to tag along on a swing through the South—when he strikes out from Nashville in a small rented car, heading southwest toward the state of Mississippi, humming through the Delta on the long flat roads, toward the town of Yazoo where the hills begin, past the cotton and the rice and the dingy green pastures where the cattle are grazing. There'll be a few stops along the way—a dinnertime visit with a liberal lawyer-friend, a strategy session with a young black activist—but his real destination lies deeper in the state. He is headed toward the homeplace down in Amite, singing country songs or telling bawdy tales, backseat driving while a friend takes the wheel. . . .

"Dammit," he says with peevish good humor, "will you *please* slow down? How you gonna see when the countryside's a blur? There're some historic sites along in here. Right over there, on up around the curve, is where ole man Tweet McKelvin used to live. He was the only Republican I'd ever *seen* til I was grown. I remember the first time an automobile ever came by his place, he said, 'My God, son, the automobiles are gonna be the ruination of this country.' God, that ole guy had it all figured out, right down to what we are talking about to-day. He didn't call it an energy shortage, but he knew . . . and then he'd want a ride into town. . . ."

He laughs and spits tobacco toward the chilly night air, and then begins to talk about his family. "Right down there," he says, "down at the turn at the bottom of the hill, that's where my daddy let me drive the old '34 Ford right into the ditch. I was going too fast, but he didn't say a word, just sat there, and when we landed, he said, 'Well, I guess there's nothin' to do but go on up to the house, eat a little supper and come back tomorrow with the chain. . . .' He never even raised his voice. How you gon' rebel against that? I tell you, he's one of the gentlest, most generous human beings I've ever known. He got it from his daddy, and he did what he could to pass it down the line."

He is rolling now, and as the stories tumble out, we pause for awhile at an ancient-looking farmhouse, tidy and green, set back from the road on Highway 24. It has a TV antenna and a fresh coat of paint, but other than that it's changed very little since Campbell's grandfather, known in the family as Grandpa Bunt, raised ten children in its four small rooms. He was a stoic Baptist deacon of determined good cheer—a small-time cotton farmer, gaunt and slightly stooped, with a sun-crinkled face and wispy gray hair that grew thinner with age.

In his later years, when the children grew up and the grandchildren came, he would lean against a stump in his barren front yard, smiling to himself at the games that they played. They were a hearty consola-tion against the tragedies of his past—against the unrelenting memories from his early years of marriage, when his first three chidren, Murtis, Claudie and little Sophia, all died within weeks of the same disease. But he came through it all with no trace of bit-terness—with a kind of dogged, undismayed understanding that the world is full of suffering and caprice, and that the mission of a man is not to add to the total.

"I remember one time," says his grandson, Will, "we were playing in the yard over there by the fence. It looked a little different back in those days, which was right during the heart of the Great Depression. The road was made out of gravel and clay, and it was farther from the house than it is today—kinda curling past us toward a thick stand of pines. We were playing tag or some such game, me and about a dozen cousins and friends, when we noticed a black man coming up the road. His name was John Walker, and we thought he was a character. He had recently been beaten for stealing a sack of corn, and some of us laughed at the way he told the story: 'Lawd, they got me nekked as a jaybird. Took a gin belt to me. Whipped me til I almost shat.' So when he came shuffling by us on this particular day, we began to taunt him: 'Hey nigger, hey nigger.' But he didn't even look up, kept his eyes pointed straight at the road, as if he hadn't noticed. But Grandpa noticed, and he called us over and said very quietly: 'Now hon'—that's what he called everybody in that way that he had—'now hon, there's no more niggers. Those days are dead. All that's left now is the colored people'."

And suddenly as you listen, it begins to make sense. You begin to understand what Campbell is about—to see why his diploma from Yale is no longer on display, and why, pasted over it on the wall above his mantel, is a certificate of ordination from East Fork Baptist—lying slightly crooked in its simple black frame, but affirming that in the eyes of his fellow believers, of people like his grandfather, he is now ordained to go and preach the gospel.

He has tried to do simply that, armed with gritty understandings of the Sermon on the Mount, of the first being last and the meek and humble emerging triumphant. And the radical causes into which it all thrust him—his strategy sessions with Martin Luther King, his prison visitations to death row killers—never seriously estranged him from most members of his family. He could always return from his travels through the South, his free-lance pastorate to the centers of turmoil, and he would know that on some level—often more instinctive than openly expressed—his father and his brothers would approve of his calling.

He usually spared them the harrowing specifics, the nerve-racking scenes in the midst of demonstrations, when he was threatened occasionally by mobs of whites or trailed by deputies in the middle of the night. But there was one particular story that he related in detail, for it was, he said, a kind of conversion—a sudden, agonizing moment of truth when his faith took on a heightened sense of clarity. He learned that a friend named Jonathan Daniel—a gentle-spirited Episcopal priest who had spoken out for civil rights in the dusty reaches of rural Alabama—had been murdered, torn apart by a shotgun blast in the slumbering, sun-baked village of Hayneville. Campbell was devastated. But in the midst of his grief, he found himself forced by his own theology to affirm that the sins of the murderer were already forgiven—that the undeserved shower of divine forgiveness rains upon us all, and that the astonishing, common-thread human opportunity is simply to accept it.

"It was a revelation," he says. But it was also something more personal than that; it was a rediscovery of the things that his grandfather knew—that in a world full of tragedy, you don't choose sides; that you can stand for what's right and yet reject condemnation for those who are wrong. So when an all-white jury freed Daniel's killer, Campbell made a point of endorsing the verdict. It was shocking news back in 1966, when he wrote in a liberal Christian quarterly, "Jonathan can never have died in vain, because he loved his killer—by his own last written words. And since he loved his murderer, his death is its own meaning. And what it means is that Tom Coleman, this man who pulled the trigger, is forgiven. If Jonathan forgives him, then it is not for me to cry for his blood, his execution. Any act on my part which is even akin to 'avenging' Jonathan's death is sacrilege. . . . For when Thomas killed Jonathan, he committed a crime against the State. When Thomas killed Jonathan, he committed a crime against God. The strange, the near maddening thing about this case is that both the offended parties have rendered the same verdict—not for the same reasons, not in the same way, but the verdict is the same—acquittal."

Later, he admits with a sort of rueful self-bemusement, "A whole bunch of my civil rights friends came to me and said, with considerable embellishment, 'Good God, Campbell, you stupid idiot, you can't go saying things like that to a bunch of rednecks. Man, that just gives 'em license. But of course, I told 'em, that's not true. What the jury told Tom Coleman was, 'You are forgiven. Go thou and kill again, if you want.' But what the gospel says, and what we are obliged to say is, 'Your sins are already forgiven you, brother. Go thou and kill no more.' That's the difference, and it's all the difference in the world."

And for those who regard such words as the ravings of a madman or the babblings of a fool (and there are many who fall into each of those categories), Campbell has a different answer. Instead of arguing the efficacy of conversions through divine compassion, he shifts his ground and attacks the alternative. "The law," he says. "We are forever arguing that people must be restrained, so we pass a law and set about enforcing it. But if the law is for the purpose of preventing crime, of securing a just and civilized society, then every wail of a siren calls out its failure. Every civil rights demonstration attests to the inability of the courts to provide racial justice. Every police chief who asks for a larger appropriation because of rising crime rates is admitting his own failure. Every time a law has to be *enforced*, then it has failed to do what we hoped it would. So what I am saying is, for God's sake, let's try something else."

He has built an organization on precisely that premise—a haphazard collection of like-minded people, ranging over the years from John Spenkelink to novelist Walker Percy. It's an otherwise ill-defined group called the Committee of Southern Churchmen, subsisting year-to-year on patched-together budgets of $30,000— most of it coming from small foundations. The committee publishes a quarterly Christian journal, with contributors ranging from Percy to Robert Coles. But its primary function is to provide a base for Campbell—a subsistence salary, a generous travel budget and a log cabin office in the hills near Nashville.

People often ask him exactly what he does, and the answer isn't easy. He listens to the problems of bewildered individuals, writes magazine articles and occasional books. The first major seller, *Brother to a Dragonfly*, was nominated for the National Book Award in 1978, and his most recent, a novel called *The Glad River*, has drawn widespread acclaim.

But one of the clearest indications of the nature of Campbell's calling occurred in 1980 when Billy Graham came to Nashville, arriving on a warm summer Saturday and sending word to Campbell that he'd like to get together. Graham was preparing for a crusade at Vanderbilt, and through an intermediary, he invited Campbell to meet him backstage—"just to get acquainted," the intermediary said.

Campbell considered it a strange invitation. He had never met Graham, though he'd tried on occasion, and he knew that their differences had been well-publicized. Some eight years earlier, at the height of the killing in Vietnam, he had written an open letter in a Christian magazine, chastising Graham for his support of Richard Nixon. And more recently than that, speaking to a convention of ministers in Graham's hometown, he had scoffed at the blandness of mass market evangelism. But despite such differences, and despite his theology, Campbell is inclined to *like* Billy Graham—to respect him grudgingly for his personal decency and for his stubborn refusal, nearly 30 years ago, to allow his crusades to be segregated racially. So he looked forward to their meeting for many of the same reasons that Graham proposed it—he wanted an opportunity to discuss their disagreements, but also to affirm that they were brothers in the faith.

It looked for awhile, however, as if it would all fall through. For as Graham preached to the multitudes at Vanderbilt, inveighing against divorce and pre-marital sex, Campbell was absorbed in his own Christian witness. He had a wedding, a baptism and a visit to death row;

then a counseling session with a troubled seminarian. And then came the funeral of Bill Jenkins, where he preached a sermon and cried with the family—cursing his lapse of pastoral detachment, while one of Jenkins's daughters, a big, friendly woman with a robust grin, patted him on the arm and consoled him gently: "Now, now, preacher, we all know how you loved Papa. You just go ahead and cry."

But the most wrenching moments came later in the week, just a few hours before he was supposed to meet Graham. He traveled to the town of Lebanon, Tenn., a medium-sized hamlet some 30 miles from Nashville, with flat-roofed stores along its downtown streets and a Confederate monument in the center of its square. And there in the shadows of early afternoon, amid the tension and humidity of a crowded courtroom, he pleaded for the life of Tyrone Bowers.

Bowers was a black man, 22 and stocky, with close-cropped hair and hard, steady eyes that stared straight ahead. Though he insisted he was innocent, five separate witnesses linked him to a murder—to the death of an amiable white man whose name was Glenn Taylor, a 41-year-old father of two and a popular figure among the people of Lebanon. According to the witnesses, Bowers admitted robbing Taylor on a cold winter midnight, leading him through a field of waist-high sage and putting six bullets in the back of his head. They said he pulled the trigger until the gun failed to fire, while his victim moaned and begged for his life.

Campbell knew Taylor and was shocked at his death. But as an opponent of capital punishment, he makes no exceptions; and when an all-white jury found Bowers guilty, Campbell agreed to testify at the sentencing hearing. He was asked to appear as an expert witness—a Christian ethicist who had studied at Yale and written extensively on the subject of justice. And the testimony began that way, with Campbell offering theological arguments and recounting his history of opposing executions—his occasional appearances at legislative hearings, his televised debates and his private pleadings with assorted public officials.

But when he acknowledged participation in public demonstrations, the character of the testimony began to change—to become less cerebral and considerably more emotional, as attorney general Tommy Thompson, tall and sandy-haired, with a penetrating mind and an overbearing style, sought to paint Campbell as an out-of-step radical. But in the jousting that followed, Campbell simply sidestepped and presented himself as something very different—a God-fearing, Jesus-loving preacher who takes it all seriously.

Thompson: So you were one of the masses in the streets that we see on television? Would that be fair to say?

Campbell: It would not be fair to say.

Thompson: Well would it surprise you to know that 85 percent of the general population is in favor of capital punishment?

Campbell: Of the general population? No sir, it would not surprise me. It may well be, sir, that we say one thing in church and another thing outside of church.

Thompson: All right, well let me ask you this. Would the fact that 85 percent of these people are for capital punishment make them any less of a Christian than you, sir?

Campbell: It would not make them any less the people for whom our Lord died.

Thompson: Yes sir. Well you are so concerned about capital punishment, I want you to look at that picture right there (showing him a photo of the dead man, his right arm folded beneath his head, mud on his clothes and six bullet holes in the base of his skull.)

Campbell: I have already looked at it, sir.

Thompson: And if I told you that the evidence in this case indicated that this was a hard-working man, 15 hours a day. . . .

Campbell: I know, I know. I was in his business many times.

Thompson: Well, what do you think would be an answer to a person who would not only rob him, but have him walk through a sage field, make him lay down, put his head in his hands, and sit there and shoot him once with a pistol, and when he started moaning shoot him five more times? What is the answer to that, Reverend?

Campbell paused before he offered a response, and for a moment it seemed as if he had nothing to say. But he did, of course, and the reaction was stunning in the small country courtroom, with the people jammed into the rough wooden pews, fanning themselves against the Tennessee heat and gazing steadily in the direction of the bench.

"Mr. Thompson," said Campbell, with his thoughts now collected, "apparently we do not know the answer to your question. *I* believe the answer is to evangelize the country in the name of Jesus Christ, so that it will simply not occur to anyone to commit the kind of violence that is shown in that picture, or the kind we are contemplating in this courtroom today. Until we do come to that kind of commitment and understanding of the Christian faith, I believe the spiral of violence will continue in this country. We have tried everything else we know to try. So I'm citing the only answer I know. I'm a Christian minister."

And in the astonishment that followed, Campbell knew that the point was made. The jury seemed absorbed in his simple proclamation, and several hours later he received word of the verdict—life imprisonment, instead of death in the chair. "The Spirit," he said. "Maybe it got loose in the Court of Mr. Caesar."

He considered telling the story to his brother, Billy Graham, for he thought it was possible that they could find a common ground, some

mutual, substantial affirmation about the gospel—that it is effective
and powerful amid the tawdriness of life, and that it's a sacrilegious
shame to bury it in sweetness. But when he arrived at the stadium at
7:00 that evening, with the choir and the crowds and the floodlight
falling on the artificial turf, he immediately understood that it would
not work. He found himself amused at his own presumption—at the
notion that he, Will Campbell, could evangelize the best-known
evangelist in the Christian world. So he simply smiled and joked and
said gracious things, and chuckled to himself at his own private
foolishness. And after basking backstage in the friendliness and charm,
he moved to the stands for the public performance—staring in dismay
at the slickness of it all. Then he shook his head sadly at what religion
has become, and laughed a little wanly when a friend turned and said:
"Let's get out of here and go get drunk."

"Well, how was it?" Brenda Campbell demanded.

She is a formidable woman of 56 years, 33 of which she has spent
with Will Campbell. She has become accustomed, she says, to the odd
array of people who stream through her kitchen—an unsuccessful
song-writer who needs a place to stay, a frightened young marine who
has run away from boot camp. But on this particular night, it was just a
pair of journalists, and she seemed more relaxed as she gave her husband a drink and informed him again in her booming Southern voice:
"I want to hear all about it."

"Well," he said, burping discreetly and settling in beside her on a
lumpy brown couch, "there ain't much to tell. He's a nice guy, but it's
easy to be nice when you're in that position. And the problem with it is
that people see how *nice* you are, and how pure you are, and they get
to focusing their attention on you. *I* even have that problem from time
to time; somebody'll read what I write or hear some sermon, and
before long they'll be callin' me up, or some seminarian will be comin'
along to write a Ph.D. on Will Campbellism. And I try to tell 'em,
'Don't do that. There's nothin' here. You don't look to me, and you
don't look to Billy, because that ain't where the Christian faith is. It
ain't in *niceness* or eloquence or even social commitment, and we seem
to have some trouble gettin' hold of that point. . . .'"

Then a writer-friend who was, as Campbell put it, "well into the
hops," cut into the soliloquy to demand a clarification: "You keep saying what the Christian faith isn't. Well, what the hell *is* it, if it isn't
those things?"

So Campbell smiled and picked up his guitar, and he began to
answer with his own graphic parable. He told a story from eleven
years ago, about a journey he made over to North Carolina—to the
town of Granite Quarry in the lush, wooded flatlands just east of

Charlotte. His purpose in going was to be with Bob Jones, then the Grand Dragon of the Ku Klux Klan, on the night before Jones was shipped off to prison. It was a strangely festive occasion, with all the kinfolk and Klanfolk gathered in the Dragon's cinder block home, telling funny stories and trying to be jolly and unconcerned. The whiskey flowed and the laughter continued until about two in the morning, when Campbell proposed communion. "Hell yes," said Jones, "let's have communion." So the people gathered in a circle, and Campbell unpacked his guitar and said: "I'm gonna sing a song that to me is the essence of the Christian faith. It's called 'Anna, I'm Takin' You Home,' and it's about a whore and a lover who forgives her and takes her home. That's what Christianity is all about—being forgiven and taken home to where you're loved." Then, strumming softly on his guitar, he began to pray.

"Lord, ole brother Bob is going off to jail for a while. We gonna ask you to kind of keep an eye on him. Lord, you know he's not a saint. And you also know that we sho ain't. But the Book tells us that's why you died. So that God and sinners could be reconciled. And we gon' drink to that and if it's all the same, we gon' sing our song in Jesus' name:

"Anna, I'm takin' you home. . . ."

CHAPTER 4

Sour Notes at the Grand Ole Opry

Sometime during the mid-1970s I became moved to write a book on country music. The origin of the idea was a 1974 magazine assignment to cover the move of the Grand Ole Opry from its old Ryman Auditorium headquarters to slick new facilities at Opryland USA. In the course of doing the story, I was struck with a curious thought: whenever we write history or try to understand a given period, we tend to look at politics—at wars, kings, presidents and upheavals. It occurred to me that we ought also to listen to music, for in America, especially, it chronicles the feelings and burdens, yearnings and disappointments that affect people's hearts.

That is a simple idea, but this article represents my own discovery of how profoundly true it is.

May, 1974

It's hard to say about Jimmy Snow, whether he's a holy man or just another of those dime-a-dozen radio God-salesmen who have made a pretty fair living off the souls of Southern white people for almost as long as men have known about the air waves. But whatever he is, it didn't much matter on the night of March 15, 1974, for the spirit was moving inside of Jimmy Snow, and there was a fire in his belly and a quiver in his voice. He knew it was his kind of crowd and knew too that there might never be another one quite like it. He was ready.

Jimmy Snow had heard the call of the Lord, he said, one cold winter night a dozen years ago, when he had found himself in his front yard, alone and on his knees, no shirt on his back, listening to voices from above. Because of that night, and because his daddy happens to be Hank Snow, a pillar of the Grand Ole Opry for decades, it fell to young Jimmy to preach the last sermon that may ever be heard in Nashville's ramshackled old Ryman Auditorium. The Ryman is a creaky, magnificent monument to a lot of things—to the conscience of Tom Ryman for one; for it was Ryman, a hard-living, liquor-dispensing riverboat operator, who had had his own encounter with the Divinity a little less than a century ago and decided to build a downtown tabernacle to celebrate.

In the years that followed, Ryman's brick and stained-glass edifice shook with the exhortations of many an evangelist, and the crowds would swarm in on muggy summer evenings to listen to Billy Sunday and the rest of them, shouting their amens and standing up for Jesus. But gradually economics got mixed into the picture, and Ryman Auditorium evolved into an entertainment center—a metamorphosis culminated in 1943 when the Grand Ole Opry chose the Ryman for its permanent quarters.

There was logic in the choice, of course. For the same people who had come to hear Billy Sunday were just as likely to come hear Hank Snow and Roy Acuff and Sam McGee. They felt comfortable there, and for upwards of 30 years they arrived in droves.

But March 15 marked the end of that era. It was the Opry's last performance in its old home, and when it moved on the following evening, the President of the United States came down to celebrate, and the crowd that was there to celebrate with him consisted not of the poor whites whose music was being performed on stage, but of the Nashville business people, who appreciated the economic possibilities if not the twanging guitars.

The night before, however, had belonged to Jimmy Snow and the country people. And in place of the President, there was Johnny Cash in his ruffled white shirt and long-tailed coat—looking like a Civil War vintage U.S. senator but singing like what he is: a man who has seen both the bottom and the top, and who was probably right at home in both places.

Cash was the closing act for Jimmy Snow's "Grand Ole Gospel Time," a popular Friday night feature of the Opry, and that night's show was one of the best. It featured the traditional gospel renditions of the LeFevres, the more upbeat compositions of a young Johnny Cash protege named Larry Gatlin, a rollicking, foot-stomping performance by country-rock singer Dobie Gray (who is one of the few blacks ever to appear on the Opry), and then the whole Cash clan.

By the time Dobie Gray was through it was late at night, and though it was cold and rainy outside, it was stuffy and humid within. The air was musty with mingled sweat fumes, and the people were tired. But they came abruptly to life, and the flash bulbs popped like a psychedelic light show when Cash appeared on stage. And when he led the entire cast through the country-folk classic, "Will the Circle Be Unbroken," even the hard-bitten newspaper reporters in the crowd had to admit they were probably seeing something special. At least a few eyes were not entirely dry.

Then Cash left the stage, and Jimmy Snow launched into his fire and brimstone Friday night message—mingling his exhortations for Jesus and America and the good old days, and forgetting, it seemed, that immortal sermons don't have to be eternal. Meanwhile, a very different scene was taking place across the alley from the Opry's backstage door—in the beer-sloshing pandemonium of Tootsie's Orchid Lounge.

Tootsie's is a typical-looking downtown dive with a garish purple front, presumably approximating the color of an orchid. In the front windows are two neon Stroh's beer signs, one of which works. Neighboring establishments include a pawn shop, a skin-flick theater, and the Magic Touch Massage Parlor. The inside walls at Tootsie's are papered with thousands of photographs and autographs of musicians, ranging in stature from Elvis Presley and Burt Reynolds to such lesser lights as Billy Troy and Ken Allen.

As its inner decor suggests, the thing that sets Tootsie's apart is its clientele. Over the years, country musicians have made it a part of their ritual to duck out the back door of the Opry House and grab a quick beer with Tootsie—rubbing shoulders in the process with the truck drivers, downtown drunks, Opry fans and other everyday beer-drinkers who are, in fact, the blood and guts of country music.

The first time I was ever a part of that scene was about three years ago, and I was with a group of a half-dozen tourists that happened to include several high-powered newspaper editors from my home state of Alabama. Our table was being attended by an enormously obese waitress, who reminded me somehow of the Wife of Bath and regaled us with a wide assortment of mildly off-color jokes. As she served the second round of beers, she placed one of them too close to the edge of the table, where it teetered precariously for a moment, then toppled neatly into one of the editorial laps. "Oops," she said matter-of-factly in her flattest cracker twang, "did I get it on your dick?"

The editor stared helplessly from his lap to the waitress and back to his lap, trying to decide what response was appropriate under the circumstances. And then with his pretensions pretty well devastated, he collapsed in helpless laughter. It was typical of the sort of ribald egalitarianism that prevails at Tootsie's, presided over by Tootsie herself—Tootsie Bess, a worldly-wise little lady, who is known around Nashville for her acts of maternal kindness toward anyone down on his luck.

Tootsie's is one of those collateral country music institutions that has nurtured the Grand Ole Opry for years. And though such things are difficult to measure, the Opry will no doubt be a little bit different now that it has moved from its old building and severed its back-alley affiliation with the orchid-colored lounge.

"Yeah, I'm gonna miss it," murmured Johnny Cash as he left the Ryman Auditorium for the last time and moved past Tootsie's back door. "I'm gonna miss it, but still I'm looking forward to the new place too."

By any objective standards of comparison, the new place is a great deal nicer than the Ryman. It is bigger; it has more comfortable seats; its acoustics are more scientifically coordinated; and it's in what would be an idyllic pastoral setting on the winding banks of the Cumberland River. The only problem is that the Opry people also plopped a large amusement park down on the same spot, and it doesn't quite fit. It's a nice amusement park: It has a hell of a roller coaster and a lot of animals and things for the kids to look at, but its connotations are far more 1970s-American than the beer-guzzling God-fearing milieu of white man's soul that used to surround the Ryman.

The Opry folks, however, seem to like it. The press kit handed out to reporters on hand for the grand opening was jammed full of quotes from various stars on the virtues of Opryland, as the new place is called: "I am very much impressed with the structure of the new Opry House," says the quote from Roy Acuff. "I think it is the greatest thing that has happened since the Grand Ole Opry was born," adds Roy Drusky. "The move will be a great thing for country music," offers Hank Snow. And so on.

No doubt the quotes are for real, but whether they are or not, nobody could deny that the Opry got off to a spectacular start in its new home. On hand among others for the dedication performance were one President, two senators, at least three governors, and a basketful of congressmen. The President, Richard Nixon, played "God Bless America" on the piano. Roy Acuff tried unsuccessfully to teach him how to Yo-yo. And the crowd, which was a Nixon crowd—not country, but spiffy, big-business, fund-raising Republican—loved every minute of it.

The Opry performers themselves were in pretty glittery form. Comedian Jerry Clower told some of his funniest, down-home Mississippi stories. Porter Waggoner was dressed in one of his gaudiest sequined suits. And blonde-haired Jeannie Sealy offered a knock-out version of "Don't Touch Me If You Don't Love Me Sweetheart," dressed at the time in a svelte, tight-fitting pants suit, with a bare midriff and the kind of plunging neckline that would have knocked many a country matron dead in her tracks from shock.

Backstage the reporters were swarming around, snatching interviews where they could, and during the course of it all, a Voice of America man cornered Minnie Pearl just outside of her dressing room. "Would you tell us, please," he said, "if you think perhaps that the Grand Ole Opry has lost its innocence?"

Minnie Pearl paused thoughtfully before answering, for contrary to her "Howdeee" public image, she is an enormously intelligent woman. "Well," she said quietly, "there are a lot of people who would argue that the Opry lost its innocence some time ago . . . back when the music started to change."

"Lordy, I reckon it has changed," echoes Sam McGee, and he should know. McGee, who is now 80, joined the Grand Ole Opry on its third or fourth radio broadcast back in 1925 when the show was still called the WSM Barn Dance and performed in a small hotel room. He still appears on the Opry nearly every Saturday night, and along with his brother Kirk and several other glib-fingered guitar and banjo pickers like Claude Lampley, Sam McGee is one of the very few early vintage Opry stars still around after 49 years.

He lives outside of Nashville on a 400-acre cattle and tobacco farm, which he still works himself. The road which leads to it winds its way randomly around the steep Tennessee hillsides, constantly and casually doubling back on itself, until finally you arrive at a rust-spattered mailbox jammed into a milk can with the words "Sam F. McGee" hand-painted on top.

Inside the sturdy stone farmhouse, the rooms are moderately cluttered with the trappings of his work—two guitars and a banjo stashed away in the living room corners, an ASCAP silver service award "for over a half-century of constant and heart-rendering contributions . . ." hung on the wall, and records strewn on the dining room table. Next to the living room fireplace is a smaller table with a Bethlehem manger scene permanently in place and an unframed, autographed picture of George Wallace leaning next to it.

On the day after the Opry changed locations, McGee leaned forward in his creaky old rocking chair and began to expound in his genial and self-effacing way on the changes he has seen. "It's just so different today," he said. "You have about 50 musicians for every one that we had back then, but you know I honestly believe the music in those days was better. You had nothing but the pure sound. Now you have all sorts of drums and amplification and all that. I don't know, I may just have an old fogy attitude, but I do know I still get a lot of letters from people asking, 'Why can't we get more of the old style country music like you play?' "

"Back then, you didn't figure to go into music as a profession," McGee continued, warming to the subject, his clear eyes taking on a sparkle as the recollections came back. "No, in those days people just played for the love of music. During those first few shows, the solemn old judge (George Hay, who originated the Opry) couldn't pay us anything because the program wasn't making enough money. We didn't care. We loved the music and we knew he would do the best he could if the program survived."

Now that the Opry is doing well enough to spend $43 million on the new Opryland complex, its executives pay McGee an average of $36 a Saturday night, and thus he still makes his living, as he always has, from farming.

He generally plays two slots on each Opry show—one as a part of a group known as the Fruit Jar Drinkers, which backs up a new-style square dance group; and the other in a featured performance with his brother Kirk. The two of them often play their original compositions, and on grand opening night at the new Opry house, they chose a quintessential country song called "When the Wagon Was New"—which celebrates a simpler time when people were in less of a hurry and when money was only a means to an end.

The McGees pioneered their own picking style, and among the more serious connoisseurs of musical talent, it is the object of considerable awe. But a few people around the Opry will tell you that among the program's executives, Sam and Kirk McGee are not exactly considered hot commercial property, and the assessment shows in a variety of ways.

For example, Sam McGee, who knows that many of his fans are older people and farmers who prefer to go to bed early, has been pleading for years for an earlier slot on the Opry, but so far he has not been successful. "I hope if I live to be old enough," he confided, "I'll get it. I think maybe I will. But we'll just have to see."

Among those who are not optimistic is Sam McGee's son Clifton, who has been appearing on the Opry for about a year, playing rhythm guitar for his father. Clifton McGee says it is awkward for him to say very much without being accused of prejudice in favor of his dad, but he can't help wondering, among other things, why the older per-formers—his father, his uncle, Claude Lampley, DeFord Bailey, Herman Crook, and the others who kept the Opry going in its early years—have never been inducted into Nashville's Country Music Hall of Fame.

It is a good question, and it has occurred to other Nashville musicians. "The old-timers self-evidently deserve it," said one. "They are certainly talented enough, and their contributions to country music are obviously sufficient for consideration. You know they will be admitted after they are dead, and yet it would be such a thrill to them if it happened while they are alive."

But the Hall of Fame, many musicians feel, is like much of the rest of Nashville's music industry: It is swayed very heavily by success that can be measured in dollars and cents, and that is something Sam and Kirk McGee haven't had much of.

And so it is that the most traditional musicians on the Opry—the people who at one time *were* the Opry—are now the hangers-on, watching country music head down new and more glamorous paths, and wondering if the old forms will die out with them.

Several years ago, a talented young Louisiana musician named Tony

Joe White composed a song entitled "A Rainy Night in Georgia." The first big hit recording of it was done by a veteran black singer named Brook Benton, and as he wailed out the plaintive lyrics about being lonesome on a rainy night, you could see in your mind an aging, nomadic black man leaning against the side of a box car with his tattered clothes and a head full of memories. This year, the song was redone—by Hank Williams, Jr., and the image is just as clear: of a white hobo traveling to who knows where on a midnight train.

You don't think of blacks when you think of country music, but in the rural South at least, the laments of Negroes and whites have covered a lot of common ground. The best of country musicians today, people like Waylon Jennings, will concede the on-going influence of blacks; and as it turns out, one of the earliest stars on the Grand Ole Opry—in fact, the first man known to have made a record in Nashville—was DeFord Bailey, a black harmonica player.

Bailey joined the Opry only a few weeks after its founding in 1925, and performed there for 16 years before he was dropped from the cast under cloudy circumstances. For the next three decades after that, he didn't perform much and made his living instead by shining shoes on a Nashville street corner. But the city fathers urban-renewed his shoe stand not long ago, and Bailey, now 74, spends his days in a housing project near the vacant lot where the stand used to be. He says he still plays his harmonica a lot—"just about the way some people smoke cigarettes."

His most popular and impressive composition, perhaps, is a tune called "Pan American Blues," in which he duplicates with his harmonica the sound of a speeding locomotive, while at the same time sounding musical. It used to knock them dead at the Opry, and the white stars like Roy Acuff now ackowledge that when they traveled, they used to take Bailey along with them in order to draw the crowds.

It is not easy to persuade DeFord Bailey to talk about the music industry that shafted him. He will sit there, dressed in his stiffly pressed blue suit, his felt hat and his spotted tie, and he will parry every question expertly—always polite, but always noncommittal, unless he has seen some concrete reason to trust you. Few writers other than a young Vanderbilt history student named David Morton have been able to establish such trust with Bailey, and when I took my own stab at it not long ago, I didn't come anywhere close.

But with Morton's help, I did manage to pull out one answer that may have shed some light on the way he thinks. Asked if he would consider performing again on the Opry stage or elsewhere, Bailey replied with a smile, "If they're talking right."

The topic of conversation he has in mind is money, and although there have been a number of negotiations on the subject in recent years, few have gotten anywhere. Bailey passed up a chance to cut an album with Pete Seeger, even though he was offered a flat fee and a royalty percentage considerably in excess of the going rate. He turned down an offer to appear at the prestigious Newport Folk Festival, and most recently, according to David Morton, Bailey was offered $2,500 to play three songs in an upcoming Burt Reynolds movie. He turned it down on the grounds that it wasn't enough.

"I don't want to give the impression that Mr. Bailey has been terribly difficult to deal with," says David Morton, who has become Bailey's friend, apologist, and unpaid manager. In fact, however, that impression is pretty close to accurate, and the reason would seem to be this: DeFord Bailey spent 16 years as one of the biggest stars on the Grand Ole Opry, and like other Opry performers, he was paid very poorly. He knows he is among the greatest harmonica players ever ("I was a humdinger," he says with a smile), and that knowledge is curiously liberating. He has nothing to prove and no apparent hunger for fame or money. If you want to hear him, you can pay his price simply as a matter of principle. If you do not want to pay his price, there are no hard feelings, but you will not hear him, and that is that.

It all sounds terribly arrogant, and it is. But most arrogance is tinged with a kind of feisty, uncertain quality, and DeFord Bailey's is not. He is one of the most polite, gentlemanly, self-bemused, and delightedly self-assured people in the state of Tennessee. He is also nobody's fool. He has learned from his own experiences, and perhaps he has learned as well from the experiences of another black Nashville singer named Cortelia Clark, whose story is one of the most tragic in the history of Nashville music.

Clark was a blind Negro street-singer who spent a good part of his life on a downtown Nashville sidewalk, rasping out the blues, while he played his guitar and sold pencils for whatever amount people chose to drop into his tin cup. In 1967, however, when Clark was an old man, a young music producer named Mike Weesner came up with the idea of having him do an album. Arrangements were made with Chet Atkins of RCA, and the album, entitled "Blues in the Street," was cut. It was a masterpiece. Critical acclaim was so high that Clark won a 1967 Grammy Award.

The only problem was that the album didn't sell. Clark made little money from it and soon found himself back on his downtown sidewalk, selling pencils, his music nearly drowned out by the on-rushing traffic.

I was a reporter for the Associated Press a couple of years after that, when Cortelia Clark was killed in a fire at his home. He was buried obscurely, at a rain-spattered funeral attended by only a few of his close friends. The poignance of it all was a little overwhelming, so I worked at some length over a story about his life, and teletyped it to the New York AP office for distribution over the national wires.

A few minutes later, the phone rang. It was the editor from New York. "Jesus Christ," he snapped in his nasal, Manhattan twang. "What do you think we're running—an obituary service for beggars?"

One person in Nashville who was particularly struck by the irony of Cortelia Clark's life was Mickey Newbury, a singer and song writer now in his 30s, who, after years of quality work, has begun to inch his way into the big time with such compositions as "The American Trilogy" and "San Francisco Mabel Joy." Newbury was raised on country music in the dusty back streets of Houston, but he is young enough to have been influenced in his musical tastes by the protest singers of the 1960s, and perhaps that is one reason he is inclined to reach for poignance and meaning wherever he can find it.

In any event, he wrote a song about Cortelia Clark, and it is one of the best of an emerging genre in country music: songs about the shared wisdom of blacks and whites in the rural South. There are other examples: Tom T. Hall's recording about a conversation with an aging black janitor who had come to see, in the course of his life, that the only things in the world worth very much at all are old dogs, children, and watermelon wine; or Don Wayne's composition about an old black woman helping a white boy come to grips with his mother's out-of-wedlock pregnancy ("a human is a human," she says, "and a saint is mighty hard to come by"); or Billy Joe Shaver's more earthy offering about an inter-racial seduction scene and the relationship that grows out of it.

One other song in that category is worth special mention because of the artist who sang it. A year or so ago, Johnny Russell, a fat and funny guitarist with a pleasant, powerful voice, turned out a song entitled "Catfish John," which told of a friendship between a young white boy and a former black slave, who was once swapped by his owner for a chestnut mare. It was Russell's biggest hit until this year, when he released a record with the absolutely on-target, good-ole-boy country title of "Rednecks, White Socks and Blue Ribbon Beer."

The song, which is set in a redneck bar, celebrates the way of life that its title connotes, and on the surface it is the sort of record that causes people like Richard Nixon to claim country music as their own kind of turf. Rednecks are simply assumed to be patriotic, red-blooded, all-American vote-fodder for conservative Republicans, and any affirmation of redneckism—which Russell's song is—is therefore assumed to be a plus for the President.

Whether or not such thoughts were in Nixon's mind at the grand opening of the new Opry house, he did in fact pick that occasion to offer one of the season's more eloquent combinations of truth and misstatement about the nature of country music.

"In a serious vein for a moment," he said, "I want to say a word about what country music has meant to America. . . . First, it comes from the heart of America. It talks about family. It talks about religion. And it radiates a love of this nation—a patriotism . . . Country music makes America a better country."

True, as far as it goes, but there is much more to it. For one thing, although some country music does talk about family, a great deal of it is about divorce, infidelity, seduction, and the seamier side of life. Some of the year's hits included Conway Twitty's "You've Never Been This Far Before," which is not even subtle; Charley Rich's award-winning "Behind Closed Doors," in which he informs the world that when the lights are turned out, his woman makes him glad he's a man, and Brenda Lee's "Don't Go Gettin' Any Wrong Ideas," which tells the story of a man who picks her up in a bar.

In addition, the patriotism of country music is not necessarily the utterly uncritical kind that Nixon has in mind. Merle Haggard may have recorded "Okie from Muskogee" and "The Fightin' Side of Me," but he also wrote "If We Make It Through December," which is a melodramatic account of a Christmastime factory lay-off. And the rednecks with their white socks and Blue Ribbon Beer that Johnny Russell sings about are anything but well-to-do, satisfied Nixonian conservatives ("We don't fit in with that white collar crowd," affirms the chorus proudly. "We're a little too rowdy and a little too loud"). And Russell himself, meanwhile, is equally willing to sing about the injustices of slavery and racial snobbery.

All such analysis, however, is a little disconcerting to most country artists, for their work is seldom deliberately political. When Tom T. Hall writes about a wounded GI returning home from Vietnam, the song can speak to both hawks and doves, because it touches a level of feeling that is universally human and beyond political abstraction. "Hell," says Waylon Jennings, "people interpret things the way they want to, and that's fine. But most of us in the business don't have enough sense to think in those terms. We'd all be nothing but rednecks ourselves if we didn't happen to have a little talent."

Which, of course, is nonsense. It may be true that Waylon Jennings is a redneck—a tough but gentle West Texas good ole boy—but you don't have to spend much time around his comfortable South Nashville house before you realize that he is anything but stupid. Like other vanguard country performers, however, his intelligence is more intuitive and poetic than it is analytical, and he doesn't waste much time on critical interpretation.

Jennings is among the more prominent of an ill-defined class of innovative country musicians around Nashville—a rough-hewn, sometimes inarticulate bunch who are serious about their music and who bristle at the still widely held assumption that country music and the Grand Ole Opry are virtually synonymous terms. Many of them have grown to regard the Opry as one of country music's more cliqueish, commercialized and unimaginative manifestations, and they are inclined to keep their distance.

A few of them, like Vince Matthews, learned the hard way. Matthews is a young, talented, but still fairly obscure song writer, who has written for such artists as Gordon Lightfoot and Johnny Cash, but who has yet to consistently crack the big time. For the past four years, he has been writing and polishing a set of original songs that are collectively titled, "The Kingston Springs Suite."

"What it is, really," he explains, "is a country opera. It is about the people in the town of Kingston Springs, Tenn., where I spent seven years, and a lot of writers and people I respect, like Shel Silverstein, have told me that it's damn good. I take that as quite a compliment, because to me Shel Silverstein is just about the best country writer around. Anyway, I went to the people at the Opry a while back and asked them to let me do the Suite out at Opryland. I had heard these stories about how Stonewall Jackson (who is a guitar-twanging distant relative of the general) drove up here in his pick up truck from Moultrie, Ga., or some place, and said, 'Here I am,' and suddenly he was on the Grand Ole Opry. Well, that may have been how it was at one time, but it isn't any more. They just looked at me like I was crazy."

Matthews and a number of other creative country musicians have come to see the Opry as the stifling culmination of the caution, conservatism, and corporate timidity that afflict country music—just as they afflict most of the nation's other major industries.

A striking example of the kind of thing that makes many performers jealous of their independence came last Christmas, when a long-time Ryman Auditorium regular named Skeeter Davis—a wide-eyed, attractive blonde whose up and down, 20-year singing career included some enormous hits in the early 1960s—displayed her penchant for gushing, unabashed sincerity and got herself banished from the Opry stage. The effusive Miss Davis had been struck by the irony of the Nashville police arresting a handful of local Jesus freaks who, with a starry-eyed seasonal zeal, had managed to irritate a number of harried Christmas shoppers with persistent affirmations that Jesus loved them. When she performed on the night of Dec. 8, 1973, Miss Davis told the applauding Opry faithful,

"I appreciate it, and a while ago I sang my record and everything. But we're having a great thing happening in Nashville—the Jesus people are here. They've been having Jesus rallies every night out at Second and Lindsey Avenue. And a while ago—this is something I just feel like I should share it; I didn't ask our manager—but they've arrested 15 people just for telling people that Jesus loves them. That really burdens my heart, so I thought I would come to the Opry tonight and sing. Here we are, celebrating Jesus's birthday. He's liable to come before Christmas, before Santa Claus does. That's something to think about. I would like to sing for ya'll this song."

When she completed her reedy-voiced rendition of "Amazing Grace," the fans applauded warmly, but when the show was over, Miss Davis was abruptly suspended for criticizing the police and infusing the Grand Ole Opry with unwanted political controversy.

All of this is to say that country music is a great deal more varied and complex than many people think it is, and some of the best and most prophetic of it is either occurring outside of the Grand Ole Opry or is given a low priority within it. But any criticism of country music's most venerated institution has to be weighed against one important fact. There is no other place in America where on a given Saturday night, country music lovers can see Porter Waggoner, Dolly Parton, Roy Acuff, Justin Tubb, Hank Snow, Marty Robbins, Sam McGee, and a dozen more all on the same show. You don't hear the fans complaining.

And if the Opry has given up some intangible quality in its move to a new and snazzier home, well the hamburger has never been quite the same since McDonald's came along. The people, however, keep on buying. That is America in the 1970s, and nothing is immune.

During the time since this piece was written, two of the principals, Tootsie Bess and Sam McGee, have died. There has also been another change. Officials at the Opry, stung by a string of bad press, seem now to attach more importance to their traditional musicians—and are more open to musical innovation as well. Whatever its flaws, the Opry remains the grand institution of country music.

CHAPTER 5

Potshots at Elvis

One of the most poignant stories I have ever covered was the funeral of Elvis Presley. Because of that experience, and because I once saw him perform on stage, I was offended in the fall of 1981 by some sensationalized attempts to tear at Presley's legacy. This article attempts to affirm his importance in American culture, exploring the diverse elements that comprise his appeal—including his radical fusion of white and black musical sounds, out of which emerged the beat of rock 'n' roll.

November, 1981

A toxicologist testified Monday that he had never found so many drugs in a body as he discovered in the remains of Elvis Presley.
—United Press International,
Oct. 20, 1981.

He could be the Pillsbury Doughboy, so fat and puffy and pillow-stuffed does he appear . . . When he faces front, or worse, turns profile, the effect is appalling.
—From "Elvis" by Albert Goldman,
copyright 1981 McGraw-Hill.

First we create them.

We build them into something much larger than life, then grow weary of admiration and begin to tear at their flaws. Hank Williams was a drunk. Martin Luther King and John Kennedy both cheated on their wives, and Mickey Mantle was rude to the fans who adored him.

So now, it seems, it's Elvis Presley's turn. Newspapers have been filled with the headlines from Memphis—how his doctor, George Nichopoulos, shot him full of drugs, presiding over his pathetic deterioration as an addict.

Simultaneously, a heralded biography—proclaimed by its publisher to be a "definitive" piece of work—is excerpted by Rolling Stone and riddled with revelations that are intended to be sensational: "Like all junkies," writes author Albert Goldman, "Elvis suffers from a paralyzed colon. Opiates immobilize the striate muscles that produce defecation.

"The abnormally large doses of laxatives that he must take to rouse his numbed gut force his body to the opposite extreme. Sometimes, he loses control of his bowels completely. Many a morning, it is necessary to strip the bed before the housekeeper arrives, lest the gossip spread through the hotel that 'Elvis Presley shits in his bed.' "

I find such passages remarkably depressing. The reason, I suppose, is that I saw Presley twice, and that was all it took to evoke a certain sympathy—a respect for his talent, and a fascination for his place in American culture.

The first time I saw him was in 1977—Feb. 20, a breezy, cold night at the Charlotte Coliseum. His fans began arriving a little after 7, streaming across the parking lot and crowding toward the doors.

Elvis himself did not appear until 10. He seemed a little thick around the mid-section and puffy about the cheeks, but splendid nevertheless, with his glittery white costume and gold chains around his neck.

For the first half hour, he mostly fooled around—posing for the flashbulbs and kissing the women who made it past the cops. But after a while, the music took hold of him. It happened on a song called "How Great Thou Art," the old gospel classic he used to hear as a boy. He sounded like Mario Lanza with soul, bending over the mike as the sweat dripped from his face, cutting loose the notes that would send chills up your spine.

You listened to that and suddenly you understood if you had never known before: Despite all the hype, the carnival hoopla generated deliberately—even perversely—by his manager, Tom Parker, Elvis Presley was no fluke.

Part of his appeal was simply his charisma—his moves and sneers and punky air of rebellion. But above all that, it was his feeling for the music, his instinctive understanding of the emotions it contained. And there were few people better at putting the feelings across.

The second time I saw him, the circumstances were different. It was six months later, and I was in a line of people that stretched for half a mile—10, even 20 abreast on a cloudy Memphis day. The line inched its way through the entrance to Graceland Mansion, up an oak-lined drive and past a lawn decked with wreaths.

There, in the doorway of his columned, brick mansion, his body lay in state, looking pale and waxen with a blue shirt, white suit and stiffly combed black hair. Women burst into tears as they passed by the casket. A few fainted or staggered to iron benches outside.

And the striking thing about the scene was that the grief was very real. For every gawker who was there, several thousand genuine mourners had assembled to pay their respects, and the poignance was of a sort that you don't soon forget.

Somehow, you knew how his death must have happened—that he

had destroyed himself in slow, painful increments—and the tragedy of the destruction added sadness to the occasion.

I guess that's what's missing from the headlines and stories out of Memphis today: a sense of poignance. Albert Goldman's biography certainly has none. The deeper you plunge into the sordid revelations, the more you are struck by a certain furtive meanness—a quality beyond voyeurism, shading into condescension.

You can find it in almost any sentence you choose. Goldman contends, for example, that Elvis emerged from "hillbilly" stock—"people incapable of . . . improving their own lot." And after a chapter called "Redneck Roots" (Would he have called it "Nigger Roots" if Presley had been black?), Goldman offers a description of Presley's high school:

"Of all the dumb activities in this dumb working-class school about the dumbest was shop: Elvis Presley's major." And he referred to one of Presley's high school friends as "a tough, aggressive, football-playing poor boy, whose ribs are visibly deformed from rickets, a disease produced by not having enough money or enough brains to eat right."

All of that is intended to destroy the Elvis myth. But the effect, of course, is precisely the reverse. For it was a reaction and a rebellion against that kind of condescension that has always been at the heart of the Presley phenomenon.

Back in 1954, he wandered into Sun Records in Memphis, an unimposing brick building on Union Street, which, at the time of his death, had become an auto body shop. In the '50s, however, it pulsated with the rhythms of that part of America—the kinds of sounds you could hear on the radio in northern Mississippi or in the Memphis housing project where Elvis spent his youth.

It was class music—country, blues and gospel—the rhythms of the Southern poor and near poor, which Presley melded into the beat of rock 'n' roll. In 1956, sipping afternoon coffee at the Piedmont Grill, a Charlotte greasy spoon with formica-topped tables and a line of booths near the window, he told Charlotte Observer columnist Kays Gary:

"Colored folks been singing and playing this music for more years'n anybody knows. They played it in the shanties all 'round Tupelo, Miss., where I got it from them, and nobody paid 'tention till I goose it up. I remember old Arthur Crudup. He'd bang the box the way I do now and I usta think if I could feel what ol' Arthur felt I'd be a music-maker like *nobody* ever saw!"

Presley seemed distracted for much of the interview. He was barely more than a kid, 21 years old, and remarkably ordinary in his priorities for the day. He grinned at the waitress and fingered the hem of her slip, then left to play pool with one of his Mississippi cousins.

But before he did, he had a few words for some critics who had panned his recent show in New York.

"Debra Paget," he said, "was on the same show. She wore a tight thing with feathers on the behind where they wiggle most. Sex? Man, she bumped and pooshed out all over the place. I'm like Little Boy Blue. And who do they say is obscene? Me! Them critics don't like to see nobody win doing any kind of music they don't know nothing about."

And, of course, he was right. The critics were shocked when he would saunter toward the mike, a waterfall of hair hanging toward his eyes and his pelvis wiggling to the screams of the crowd. But the disapproval was essential, for it helped make him a rebel—a sensational cult hero with at least two followings: the nation's young, and the people who came from his own economic background.

Youth and class. Both ingredients defined his career, and both could be felt when it ended—in the mood of the crowd that assembled for his funeral. It was a peculiar mood, one that seemed to mingle both triumph and grief.

At 11:30, for example, on the night before the service, some 2,000 people were huddled in the rain, keeping resolute vigil outside of Graceland. Suddenly, Caroline Kennedy—the daughter of the late president—emerged from the mansion. With TV cameramen in hot pursuit, she made a dash to her car.

She was in town to cover the story for a New York paper, but the crowd didn't care what her reasons were. For those who swarmed around her, her presence was symbolic. And as she unlocked her car—her fingers trembling with the anxiety of the moment—a white Memphis teenager and his black companion exchanged rebel yells and soul brother handslaps.

"OOO-eee," they exclaimed. "Caroline Kennedy!"

The implication seemed clear enough. For whatever reasons, a member of one of the world's richest families had come to pay tribute to one of their own.

All that is heady stuff, but there was one final ingredient in the Presley phenomenon. It was the promotional genius of Col. Tom Parker, a frumpy carnival huckster who set about in 1955 to transform Elvis from a promising young singer to an American institution.

"I didn't tell him what to record, and he didn't tell me how to promote," says Parker. "He'd say, 'The Colonel will let 'em know I'm coming.' "

And so Parker did. He took all the talent, as well as the charisma and rebellion, and after Presley moved from Sun Records to RCA, he got him on TV and negotiated rich contracts for a string of lousy movies.

But as the money poured in and the fame began to mount, Presley was trapped under the weight of it all. In the end, of course, it crushed him. He was, at his core, a rather ordinary person—not especially well-equipped to handle his own genius, much less the excesses that it began to produce.

"Sure it got to him," says his friend Joe Moscheo, now a Nashville music executive. "There's an old Indian saying, 'Walk a mile in my shoes.' He had a lot of problems, but you can't take his accomplishments away from him."

CHAPTER 6

Rock 'n' Roll, Country and George Hamilton IV

Over the past 25 years, popular music has taken a lot of turns in America, and George Hamilton IV has been there for most of them, including the beginnings of rock 'n' roll, the folk music rebellions of the 1960s and the various evolutions and mutations of country music. Unlike many performers, including some who are more famous, he has reflected very carefully on the role that music plays in American life.

December, 1981

His career, at the least, has been filled with contradictions—a peculiar reluctance and flirtation with fame, a kind of gee-whiz humility in everything he says, and an absolute delight in the recognition he has known. He has been a teenage idol and a country music super-star, a fixture on the late '60s folk music scene. His first gold record was in 1956, and more than 40 albums later, he had another one in 1979. He has been a TV regular in half a dozen countries and a 20-year member of the Grand Ole Opry. But there is also this: in most of America, including his home town of Charlotte, N.C., there are not a lot of people who could tell you his name.

It was a sultry summer morning, and George Hamilton IV was hurrying to get ready. He was absorbed in the packing and the last minute details, but wallowing just a little in the irony and guilt. It was Budapest this time—a headline performance in the first country music festival ever held in Hungary. He was excited, of course, just as he had been in 1974 when he became the first country singer to tour the Soviet Union.

"It's rocking chair stuff," he offers with a smile. "Something to tell your grandchildren about."

The problem is that Hamilton doesn't have any grandchildren. He does have a wife, a daughter and a couple of college-age sons, and they are the source of a monumental ambivalence, an air of apology about what he does for a living. Hamilton is away from home too much, and

he feels it keenly. From January to May in 1981, he toured the British Isles—61 cities over the five-month period. Then it was off to New Zealand for the third time in a year, then Hungary and England, and for most of December he'll be in Belfast.

He'd like to perform a little closer to home, and occasionally he does. In August, he drew a thousand people at a church barbecue in the North Carolina mountains. And a couple of months later, approximately that many turned out in Charlotte. But the crowds are mostly small and the offers widely scattered. It's been more than six years since his last American hit and even longer since his really big records, songs such as "Abilene" and "Early Morning Rain."

Nevertheless, as Hamilton reflects on it all—and he's inclined to introspection more than most country singers—he wouldn't make many changes if he had it to do over.

"It's been a double-edged sword," he admits a bit ruefully, a sheepish smile spreading across his face, which is a handsome face, with a neatly trimmed beard showing a few flecks of gray. "There's a guilt syndrome," he explains, "about being an absentee husband and father. But in being a performer—and in your private moments you'd like to think of yourself as an artist—there's a deep-seated need to do what you do. I enjoy it so much. I need it so much. It's hard to imagine things another way."

His career began in Chapel Hill in 1956. Hamilton was a student at the University of North Carolina, a shy and skinny freshman who didn't quite fit. He was popular enough in an odd sort of way—chiefly, he assumed, because he could sing country songs and play the guitar, and his buddies at the frat house were amused by his talent.

Those were the heady, early days of Elvis Presley's rock 'n' roll, and although Hamilton was impressed with its energy and excitement, he was hooked nevertheless on the twang of country music. His ambition was to perform at the Grand Old Opry, and less than four years later that's what he was doing.

In between, however, he reluctantly joined the ranks of the rockabilly idols—a teenybopper-heartstopper, criss-crossing the country, hanging out with Chuck Berry, Dion, Sam Cooke and Buddy Holly. He had wandered into the studios of UNC's campus radio station, settled his gangly frame behind a microphone and cut a whiny teen ballad called "A Rose and Baby Ruth." Hamilton didn't even like the song. But he released it on a little Chapel Hill label called Colonial Records. Soon, Fred Foster—then a talent hunter for ABC Paramount records—heard Hamilton's song and decided to buy the rights for ABC.

Foster's bosses were appalled.

"They thought it was terrible," says Foster, now top executive with Nashville's Monument Records. "But I had gotten this call from Buddy Deane who was a DJ at WITH radio in Baltimore. Buddy said, 'I just played this record by a kid from North Carolina, and the phones went crazy.' So I went over and heard the song, and I said, 'I don't know, man, I've heard better records.' And Deane said, 'I'm tellin' you, it's a hit.'

"Well, my immediate boss was named Larry Newton. He was a big, gruff guy who intimidated everybody, and I knew he'd pick the record apart. So I called Sam Clark, who was president of the label, and I got his permission to buy it for ABC.

"When Newton finally heard it, he called me up and said, 'You're a sick man, Foster, a sick man.' He always said everything twice. He said, 'That's the worst piece of crap I ever heard, the worst I ever heard.' So I said, "Look, Larry, if it doesn't go, you got my job. But it it does go, I want a raise.' "

It went, of course. The record sold more than a million copies, landed Hamilton on network television and vaulted him onto package tours with other teen rockers.

"We all hit it off well," Hamilton says of his rockabilly buddies. "We were all in the same age group, and we were all scared as heck. But soon we began to notice some differences, some real cultural gaps in terms of who our heroes were. Some of the Northern kids—Fabian, Frankie Avalon, Paul Anka and some others —were all really into the Italian singers, like Sinatra or Tony Bennett. I tended to gravitate to the Southern kids—Buddy Holly, Gene Vincent, especially the Everly Brothers—who were still hung up on Hank Williams.

"It was almost like the kids from the North were trying to 'rock' Frank Sinatra, while the kids from the South were rocking Hank Williams. And then there were the black singers, which was really a revelation. I toured with Chuck Berry in Australia in 1959, and Chuck was an intellectual. He used to quote Shakespeare a lot. But he also had a little chip on his shoulder. He said, 'The difference between me and you, White Boy, is that when you were there in Nashville diggin' the Grand Ole Opry, you got to sit inside. I had to stand out in the alley.' Sam Cooke was different. He was a really gentle guy, very perceptive and decent, but like Chuck Berry, he liked country music a lot.

"From all of that, you started to sense something about our common roots. It made me think. I came from suburban Winston-Salem. I was a Kappa Alpha at Chapel Hill, and the hero of our fraternity was Robert E. Lee. There were just a lot of things that I hadn't thought about. So we'd tour together and start feeling like we were friends, like it didn't matter as much who was black and who was white. And then we'd hit the South. The bus would drop the black stars off at some rundown lit-

tle hotel on the black side of town, and that created some weird feelings. This was 1958, man, and I wasn't quite ready to say, 'Hey, drop
me off at the black hotel.' But I also knew it wasn't right."

Such memories dominate Hamilton's recounting of his teen idol
days. He doesn't particularly talk about the music he was making, for
he saw it, even then, as far too syrupy and short on substance. So in
1959—while his rock 'n' roll career was still going strong—he decided
to make a change. He headed for Nashville, and by 1960 he had sung
his way into a spot on the Grand Ole Opry. He cut a string of country
hits, peaking in 1963 with a folky ballad called "Abilene," which made
its way into the country Top Five, then crossed to the pop charts and
made the Top Twenty.

There had been some major doubts among country fans when
Hamilton first came to Nashville. But he was convincing when he sang
country songs, and he was so engaging—so exceptionally nice—that it
didn't take them long to embrace him as their own. But after "Abilene"
he seemed to grow restless once again in his musical inclinations. He
found himself listening to the '60s folk singers—people like Pete
Seeger, Bob Dylan and Joan Baez. They sang the old British folk songs
that had been a part of Hamilton's family for a couple of hundred
years—mingling the ancient ballads with those of newer vintage, protest songs about the problems of America.

Hamilton liked the mix, and he began recording songs by Dylan,
Leonard Cohen and especially Gordon Lightfoot. In 1967, he cut Joni
Mitchell's "Urge for Going," becoming the first artist in any field of
music to put out a hit with a Mitchell composition. But those were
strange times. America was caught up in a war, domestic violence and
all the polarization that went along with both—and country music,
with its legions of All-American, God-fearing fans, was clearly iden-
tified with the conservative side of the chasm.

Merle Haggard was going strong with "Okie from Muskogee" and
"The Fightin' Side of Me"—records extolling patriotism and denouncing all the long-hairs who were tearing at the country. And here was
George Hamilton IV consorting with the folkies, the balladeers who
were marching in the front ranks of protest.

It was about that time that Marty Robbins, a smooth country
crooner with staunch conservative inclinations, cornered Hamilton
backstage at the Opry one night and, without a lot of subtlety, began
to question his patriotism. Hamilton tried to respond in his own gentle
way—to explain that music runs deeper, touches something more
basic, than political storms that come and go with time. He knew that
his answer had been poorly understood, but he felt driven somehow to
do what he was doing. In 1968, he appeared at the Newport Folk
Festival, sharing the stage with Joan Baez and Janis Joplin. The same

year he did a benefit concert for Robert Kennedy's presidential campaign —responding to an emergency call from a Kennedy supporter.

It was a snowy March night, and Kennedy was scheduled to speak in Nashville before 10,000 people at Vanderbilt University. But he was late. He had been delayed in Birmingham, and it would be at least two hours before he arrived in Nashville. The sponsors of the speech were searching for somebody to entertain the crowd. Plenty of country singers would have been eager to do it—if the speaker had been Richard Nixon or even George Wallace. But Kennedy, with his ringing affirmations about the rights of the poor, his liberal understanding of the problems of America, was another matter. So the phone rang at Hamilton's west Nashville house, and one of Kennedy's supporters, a Vanderbilt student whom Hamilton had never met, carefully explained the problem.

"Oh," said Hamilton, "I'm really very flattered, but I just couldn't do it. I mean all those people don't want to hear a country picker."

"Well," said the student, "if it makes you feel any better, you're all we've got."

So Hamilton agreed, and for the next couple of hours, he entertained the Kennedy partisans with a barrage of country songs. His pleasant tenor voice, with just the barest hint of nasality and flatness, echoed strongly off the gymnasium walls. The crowd, which was a Kennedy crowd and not at all steeped in an appreciation of country music, applauded him warmly.

It was during those late '60s years that a basic truth began to dawn on Hamilton: in his own Mr. Nice Guy way, despite his three-piece suits and his amiable demeanor, he's an incurable nonconformist—caught up perpetually in a grass-is-greener restlessness, a refusal to fit in wherever he happens to be. When he was a rock 'n' roll star, he wanted to sing country music. When he made it in Nashville, he began to sing folksongs. And yet through it all, he has refused to abandon his basic country tastes.

The result has been two-fold. First, he has made some new fans. His affiliation with such Canadian performers as Gordon Lightfoot and Joni Mitchell helped him develop a massive following in that country. By the mid-'70s he had his own weekly television show in Canada, which was soon syndicated in England, South Africa, Hong Kong and New Zealand. He became one of the most popular performers in the British Isles, appearing regularly on the BBC. He was the first country star to tour the Soviet Union, interspersing his concerts with lectures at the University of Moscow, and he has hosted dozens of country festivals in England, Denmark, Hungary and New Zealand.

"George Hamilton IV is the international ambassador of country music," writes Bob Powel, editor of a London magazine called *Country*

Music People. "He is undoubtedly the person who has done most to spread country music to lands where, in the past, it was met with suspicion and cynicism."

At home, however, the story is different. Hamilton's emphasis on his overseas career has become intertwined with his indifference to trends (his refusal, for example, to shed his three-piece suits for urban cowboy denims). The result is a startling lapse of popularity. His last big hit, "She's a Little Bit Country," was a decade ago, and he hasn't had a chart record in America since the middle 1970s.

So once again, the ambivalence has set in. He's delighted with his overseas success ("I'd really rather be performing in Hungary than at Billy Bob's in Ft. Worth, even if it covers four football fields and has live bulls instead of mechanical ones."), but he finds himself longing for some home front success, and in order to pursue it, he's considering several options. One is a gospel album—but not, he says, a saccharine collection of mindless Jesus anthems. "I'd like to touch on some of the social implications of Christianity," he explains. "Jesus in many ways was a pretty disturbing man."

Meanwhile, he broods periodically over his absentee status as a husband and father. He spends about as much time overseas as he does at home, and even when he's not on the road he finds himself restless—pacing through his comfortable, tree-shaded house near the small town of Matthews, N.C., wondering what to do with his midday hours.

"I know I get a little hard to live with," he says. But Tinky Hamilton, his college sweetheart and wife of 23 years, understands how it is. She may wish sometimes that he had decided to be a banker or maybe to sell real estate in the towns around Matthews. She knows, however, that it wouldn't have worked. For Hamilton at heart is a restless hillbilly, and despite all the ambivalence that occasionally besets him, he's been fortunate enough to make a living at his hobby, to see the world, and to come to his own deeply personal understanding of the role of music in the culture of America.

CHAPTER 7

The Cheerful Obsessions
of Arthur Smith

*On his home turf in the Carolinas, Arthur Smith is a legendary performer, best
known for composing the bluegrass hit, "Dueling Banjos." He is also, I think, an
American success story—a determined, millionaire refugee from the mill-town South,
who has built for himself a very colorful life. The cornerstones of it are his talent, his
old-fashioned understanding of the Christian faith and his candid obsession with the
art of making money.*

November, 1981

It was a chilly Friday morning at Little River Inlet. The moon was
still high, throwing cold, mottled light through the water oak leaves.

Off somewhere near the edge of the campground, where the trees
give way to the dank-smelling marsh, a radio sputtered out the music
of George Jones. The pathos of the lyrics mingled with the static, the
hard twang of the voice rising and falling over the muffled conversations:

"Has it really been a year since the last time I seen her? My God, I
could swear it was 10. . . ."

About 6:30, Arthur Smith rolled to a stop in his El Camino pickup,
dusty and blue, and occupying a far different place on the automotive
spectrum from the shiny twin Cadillacs he used to share with his wife.

Smith smiled and disembarked briskly with his buddy, George
Beverly Shea, a kindly bear of a man who has spent much of his life at
Billy Graham crusades, bestowing baritone renditions of "How Great
Thou Art." Shea and Smith go back a long way. To be precise, they
met on another October morning, this one in 1947, just a few minutes
before 8:15. Smith was doing a live country music show on WBT
radio, playing guitar on Charlotte's 50,000-watter, and Shea was in
town for Graham's first crusade.

"We tried to give Billy and Bev some publicity," Smith explains, the
words rolling out in a rich molasses drawl, the voice deep and friendly
with a mill-town twang.

85

Smith tries to be modest about his various achievements, including such matters as his early boosts to Graham. But you have to work at humility when you've had lots of famous friends or a million-selling record, or when you've written a song like "Dueling Banjos."

Such things can hook you on success and recognition, not to mention money. And although Smith handles the addictions with considerable grace and charm, they have been a part of his life for most of four decades.

During that time, he has made himself a kind of one-man conglomerate—combining his guitar-picking skills and his businessman's acumen in the cheerful, frank and successful pursuit of money.

Always, and most importantly, he has been a musician—an expatriate of Kershaw, S.C., who signed a recording contract with RCA, moved to Charlotte, and has lived in the city ever since. He has toured with Hank Williams, won a $200,000 legal settlement from Warner Brothers Inc. and handled the business affairs of Johnny Cash.

He has been a regular on nationwide radio, hosted more than 4,000 television programs and operated a Charlotte recording studio in which the performers have ranged from James Brown to Lester Flatt.

He has made a hobby of dabbling in politics, sometimes behind the scenes, sometimes in the forefront. He was among North Carolina's leading opponents of liquor-by-the-drink and, more recently, served as cochairman of Gov. Jim Hunt's North Carolinians for Good Roads committee.

To recent arrivals in the area who have seen him on TV, doing his amiable endorsements of Ford cars or Bost Bread, he seems a drawling throwback to an earlier time in the South. But he is not. At age 60, he is just getting started, investing his millions in a variety of enterprises—from making satellite receivers for cable TV to staging fishing tournaments at Little River Inlet.

And in recent weeks, it has been the fishing that absorbs him. This year's Arthur Smith King Mackerel Tournament—the fifth he has hosted—drew 846 boatfuls of contestants and resulted in 5 tons of mackerel being plucked from the Atlantic.

"Just look at that sight," said Smith, on the tournament's opening day. As he spoke, he was maneuvering his 42-foot, $250,000 Hatteras cruiser through the Little River channel, which winds near the border of North Carolina and South Carolina.

He was trailed by a bobbing armada, little white boats with outboard motors, bouncing over the wakes of assorted inboards, heading for open seas and the deep shoals of mackerel. Smith grinned at the spectacle, a crinkly little smile that deepened the lines in his face. "Of course," he admitted with a sudden change of expression, a brief somber nod, "I haven't broken even on this thing yet. It usually ends up costing us about $10,000."

While Smith can afford it, he never takes it lightly when he drops that amount of cash. He is shrewd and skillful at his calling in life, which he will define for you happily with one simple sentence: "Basically," he explains, "I just love making money."

This is how he does it.

Back in 1976, it occurred to him that bluegrass music had become a hot commercial item. Fans flocked to live performances—gathering at festivals like the Old Time Fiddlers' Convention in Union Grove, choking the highways and spreading across the countryside, cheering like maniacs when the pickers cut loose.

Understanding such things, Arthur asked himself a question: Why not try to sell them some records? So he began talking to Martin Hearle, a music executive from Los Angeles, and the result was CMH—a new record label for bluegrass artists. Smith bought 20% of the stock and became a vice president.

He set about signing the best artists in bluegrass—Lester Flatt, Don Reno, the Osborne Brothers. All of them soon began recording in Charlotte, maneuvering their cars and tour buses through the snarl of traffic on Monroe Road, to Arthur Smith Studios, where CMH Records had rented them some time.

There, with Smith acting as producer and backup musician, they churned out their albums—often choosing songs written by Smith. And some artists, like Don Reno, began writing new songs for the catalogue of Clay Music, Smith's publishing company.

After a while, you begin to get the picture: Arthur Smith has developed a tidy music empire. Every time he went into the studio with Lester Flatt or Reno, he wore a nice array of hats—producer, composer, record executive, publisher—and he was being paid handsomely for all of those services.

Nor is that the end of it. He has an agreement with movie producer Earl Owensby of Shelby, N.C., to compose sound tracks for his films. He produces a steady stream of jingles for radio and television, as well as three syndicated radio shows—for himself, Johnny Cash and George Beverly Shea.

Until earlier this year, he also produced his own half-hour television show, syndicated from Charlotte and carried at its peak by 72 stations. Recent guests ranged from Bob Hope to Johnny Cash, but Smith decided to stop production after about two decades "because it got to the point where it wasn't real fun."

He is reluctant to talk about his profits. But if you poke through his files you can find some indications. In the first four months of 1981, for example, 37 of his songs were played on the radio on six continents.

That earned him $16,336.56. He says he averages maybe $50,000 a year from such overseas royalties.

That, of course, is a tiny fraction of his revenue—a nice little trickle that amounts to pocket change. But his total music earnings, whatever they are, are merely what he uses to prime the pump—"investment capital," says his son, Clay Smith, that he uses in his quest to make serious money.

"We have quite a varied portfolio," Arthur concedes modestly, using the royal plural as he discusses his investments. He is seated behind a cluttered metal desk, looking amiable and relaxed in an open-necked shirt, his gray hair curling near the tops of his ears.

Smith operates out of an office in southeast Charlotte, tucked away behind his house in a grove of spindly pines. The house is made of white-painted brick, and you can tell from driving past that it's worth a lot of money. But there is nothing about his office that suggests ostentation—just a buffed gold carpet and thrifty office furniture, a guitar and a banjo leaning against the wall.

"I never had the desire to amass a lot of wealth," says Smith. "But the process of *making* money, I love it. I really do."

He settles back and begins warming to the subject, the words tumbling out slowly, fondly, with a kind of Andy Griffith cadence, each long vowel stretched into a couple of syllables.

"I don't particularly like the word 'millionaire,' " he says, explaining with a perfectly straight face that, "When you really get down to it, a million dollars is not a lot of money anymore.

"I don't have any idea what I'm worth," he continues. "With the fluctuations in the economy, I don't think there's any way to know. In our portfolio, we have industrials, municipals, utilities, stocks and bonds; real estate and holdings in family businesses. Thank the Lord, we've never had a problem with cash since we started in business."

He pauses for a minute, then shifts the subject slightly: "You know, on your way through life, you go through stages. Once I felt like Dorothy—that's my wife—I felt like she and I should have twin Cadillacs. I drive an El Camino pickup now, a '75 with 82,000 miles on it. Just so I get where I want to go. My wants are simple—fried chicken, banana puddin' and a comfortable bed."

To really understand him, it helps to go back to Kershaw in the 1920s, where he was the third of five children in a tightly knit family. His father, Clayton Smith, was a loom fixer at Springs Mills.

Back then, says Smith, textile wages weren't impressive. But the mills did what they could to build a sense of community, using such devices as a semipro baseball team and always a band—a 20-piece collection of local musicians, given to brassy renditions of patriotic anthems.

Clayton Smith was the bandleader, a capable violinist who indulged the musical aptitudes of his eager middle son—teaching him first the trumpet, then the mandolin and fiddle. By the time he hit his teens, Arthur had begun his own radio show, performing live on WOLS in Florence, S.C. In 1934, he signed a recording contract with RCA, and he was on his way. He was 13.

He already had begun to show an interest in money, and when he hit the 10th grade at Kershaw High, where he was to graduate as valedictorian, he began to make loans to friends—maybe 75 cents, for which he expected repayment of a dollar.

The sums were modest, but the interest rates were tidy, and by the time his music revenues began to roll in, Arthur's instinct for profits was fairly well developed. Still a teenager, he began to play the stock market, and, as he remembers it today, "I did pretty well from the very beginning."

He recorded steadily for RCA until World War II, and the direction of his life has never varied.

"I think Arthur decided there was more to life than working in a mill," says Grand Ole Opry singer George Hamilton IV, who has known Smith for years. "And I think he knew music could be his ticket out."

In 1942, Smith joined the Navy and was stationed near Washington as the war wound down. While there, he began recording for a little label called Super Disc Records, owned by Irvin and Izzie Feld, brothers who later became proprietors of Ringling Brothers and Barnum & Bailey Circus.

In 1945, Smith went into the Washington studio, and, backed by Charlotte musicians Roy Lear and Dan White, he cut a bouncy instrumental called "Guitar Boogie." The record sold 3 million copies, crossing the line between country and pop, and there are people who say it was a forerunner of rock 'n' roll.

One of those people is ex-Beatle Paul McCartney.

Last Sept. 8 in London, McCartney was working at Air Studios in the heart of downtown, doing keyboard tracks for an upcoming album. He stopped for a minute to greet an old friend, Joe English, who used to be the drummer in McCartney's group, Wings.

English was wandering around London with another musician, Charlottean Tim Smith, the 23-year-old nephew of Arthur Smith. "Let me shake your hand," exclaimed McCartney when he and Tim were introduced. And he quickly rummaged through a case of old records, plucking out an original of "Guitar Boogie."

Among people in the music business, Arthur has long had an imposing reputation. In the late 1940s, for example, MGM records began to build a roster of country acts. The first person they called was Bob Wills, the innovative Texan and master of western swing. The second was Smith—and only later did they sign a skinny Alabamian by the name of Hank Williams.

"But ole Hank took over," Smith concedes with a smile.

As MGM headliners, Hank and Arthur did a lot of dates together, working big amusement parks in Maryland and Pennsylvania. But Williams died in 1953, expiring at age 29 from the accumulated effects of alcohol and drugs.

Smith recorded a tribute to him—a tear-jerking recitation that was a rousing success. In truth, however, they were never very close. "Hank," says Arthur, "was never a fun guy. He was just down all the time. Whisky depressed him. Dope depressed him. Nothing got him high."

Smith says he spent about 12 years with MGM, recording maybe 200 songs. Most were instrumentals, but one was a novelty tune called "Red-Headed Stranger," which Willie Nelson resurrected in 1975, choosing it as the title song for the album that made him a superstar.

Throughout the '50s, Smith worked out of Charlotte, doing radio shows for WBT and CBS, then moving into television with WBTV. One day in 1955, he went into the old downstairs studio at WBT and after picking up his tenor banjo he turned to Don Reno, who was playing the 5-string, and told him simply: "You just follow me."

The result was "Feudin' Banjos." It was a solid hit at the time and became even more important later when Warner Brothers retitled it "Dueling Banjos" and used it as the theme for the movie "Deliverance." There was one little hitch, however. They failed to give Smith any credit or royalties.

So when the movie appeared in 1973, Smith called the Warner offices to talk about the problem. As he remembers it, it took him a couple of weeks to reach the company's lawyer—to convince the secretaries out in L.A. that this slow, drawling voice from the other end of the continent belonged to somebody they ought to reckon with.

When he finally got through, Smith says, the lawyer told him, "Mr. Smith, you haven't got the time or money to take Warner Brothers to court."

"So I told him," says Smith, " 'Sir, I do have the time, and I b'lieve I can get the money.' "

Smith's case was overwhelming. He had original recordings, a valid copyright and the character testimonials of other people in the business. "I told the opposing lawyer," says Nashville record executive Fred Foster, " 'If Arthur Smith told me he wrote "The Star Spangled

Banner," I'd believe him. I might not know quite how it was possible. But I'd know it was true.'"

Faced with all that, Warner Brothers agreed to settle as the case went to court. The settlement was around $200,000, which paled beside the royalties that began to flow in. And when it was over, Smith was able to affirm with a smile: "Even my wife was pleased."

During the '60s and '70s, he cut back on performing. He was still on television and still recorded albums, but his singles were rare and seldom very successful. As he said of one record in 1977, "It started sellin' slow, and then it kinda tailed off from there."

His business ventures were another matter. He dabbled successfully in grocery stores, restaurants and, most recently, electronics.

Still, his basic craft was always music, and one of his most profitable enterprises was his recording studio. He sold 90% of his interest in it in 1981—for more than $500,000, he says. But while he owned it, some famous people came through: Roy Orbison, Johnny Cash, George Hamilton IV. Even James Brown, the flamboyant soul singer with the conked-back hair, brought his entourage to Arthur's in 1965 and recorded a raspy hit called "Papa's Got a Brand New Bag," which reached No. 8 on the national pop charts.

But perhaps the most incongruous scene occurred about three years ago. David Allen Coe, the outlaw's outlaw of country music, a rhinestoned ex-con with a flair for the outrageous, strolled into Smith's and demanded with a smirk: "Where are the women? I got the drugs."

In fact, Coe was joking, and Smith thought it was funny. But Arthur's friends wince when they hear the story, for they regard Smith as a believer in the most old-fashioned virtues. Not only does he avoid illegal drugs, but he even opposes the use of what he calls "beverage alcohol." He's a family man, happily married for 40 years and strongly inclined to keep his life under control.

"Discipline," he asserts, "is the most important word in the Christian vocabulary."

And Arthur is a Christian. He found Jesus in Kershaw's Second Baptist Church, which he attended regularly on the prodding of his mother. And when he began seeing wife-to-be Dorothy Byars as a high school 10th grader, his attendance became even more faithful in an attempt to match hers.

"I've never had any serious religious doubts," he says. "I believe the Bible is literally true, inerrant. People say, 'These are different times. Things have changed. It's OK to do this or that. It's OK for divorced preachers to hold pastorates. Everybody's doing it.' Well, it still don't make it right. The moral law of God has not changed one iota and never will."

As you might expect, Smith can be stubborn when it comes to his principles. He has had a share of verbal collisions with Henry Crouch, the pastor at Providence Baptist Church, where Smith is a deacon. Crouch is a fairly tough man, big and overbearing and inclined to liberal stands on such social issues as poverty and world hunger. Smith has let him know he doesn't approve.

"I disagree with any preacher that preaches a social gospel," Arthur says. "Carry a family a turkey, and it'll make you feel good. That's not what religion is about. If we try to point a soul to Christ and we come upon human needs, certainly it is our responsibility to try to meet them. Still, the commission of the church is to win people to Christ. It was not formed to alleviate human suffering, but to give people eternal life."

There are those who will argue—though few of them publicly—that the heart of Smith's theology is a millionaire's indifference to a world of human suffering. But even his critics rarely question his sincerity, for his zealousness is more than a matter of lip service.

He supports 20 missionaries scattered around the world. He contributes to such humanitarian causes as the Christian Rehabilitation Center for Charlotte-area derelicts—and occasionally his principles have even cost him in business. After he once invested in a motel chain, he discovered that his partners planned to install lounges—for the purpose, of course, of serving "beverage alcohol." He decided to pull out.

"Cost me $80,000," he says, with a rare memory for such things.

So in the end what you have is a peculiar sort of fellow: His life these days is far removed from the mill-town South, the working class environment that he fled through his music. But in some fundamental ways he has carried along his origins—the old-fashioned righteousness on which he was raised.

And he is also, you can't help but notice, very pleased with himself.

"I look at the talent side of our business, the production side and the bottom line as well," he concludes. "Had I given all my attention to any one thing, I think I could do it as well as it's ever been done. But I can't do one thing. I gotta be busy. And I want to do things I can make a buck at."

CHAPTER 8

Cousin Willie

Throughout the 1960s, Willie Nelson was a staple on the country music scene—a highly successful song-writer whose ballads were recorded by everybody from Patsy Cline to soul-singer Joe Hilton. But in the early 1970s, he became a star in his own right—carried to prominence by his talent, but also by something else as well. His music became caught up in the social and political currents that were affecting his audience—a national impulse toward reconciliation after a decade that included Vietnam and Watergate and also a concern with roots. Willie was, for a time, still another example of the significance of music in American life.

February, 1976

It might have happened anyway, even if Willie Nelson's house hadn't burned, but probably not in the same way. For as the flames licked into the autumn Nashville night back in 1971, it was the crowning point in a decade of frustration for Nelson, a highly successful songwriter who always thought he could make it as a performer but could never persuade the bigwigs down on Music Row.

So as the flames crackled around him, he darted into the house, salvaged a pound of top-grade Colombian marijuana, and pointed his car in the direction of Texas. He was born there back in 1933 in a little windswept town called Abbott. Like most expatriates from the dusty reaches of the Lone Star state, he had never quite gotten it out of his system—even when things were going well and he was writing classic country songs such as "Crazy," "Hello Walls," and "Ain't It Funny How Time Slips Away."

Even in the best of times, Nashville and Willie just weren't meant for each other somehow, and when he got back to Texas and began sorting things out, he caught the fever again and decided to stay. Within a year, he found himself a kind of godfather figure in one of the most important developments, both musically and socially, in the latter-day evolution of rock and country music.

The development is the emergence in Texas of a musical form that goes by a variety of labels: progressive country, redneck rock, and several others that are used less often. But whatever you choose to call

it, it is essentially a fusion of rock and country sounds—and more importantly, of rock and country audiences—that comes after a decade of polarization over everything from the length of hair, to the color of the skin, to the ardor of competing ideology.

Slowly, in the past few years, the fusion presided over by Nelson and a handful of others has begun to spread, riding an impulse toward reconciliation and rippling westward in the direction of the coast, then eastward toward cities like Nashville, Atlanta, Charlotte, and Philadelphia. The most tangible manifestations of the spread have been Willie Nelson's "Blue Eyes Crying In The Rain" and Michael Murphey's "Wildfire," a pair of hit singles which succeeded in both pop and country markets and between them have sold well over a million records.

But there are other manifestations as well: the rabid, packed-house followings of a hard-core country-rocker named Jerry Jeff Walker, the critical acclaim for the country-flavored big band innovations of a group called Asleep At The Wheel, and the emerging popularity of a new public television series, "Austin City Limits," which features the cream of the Texas crop and is shown in 116 markets from coast to coast.

There is a kind of metaphorical logic in the fact that Austin, a bubbling college town and capital city of 300,000 people, would find itself at the center of the ripple. For Austin, says Michael Murphey, the gentle spirit and resident intellectual of the city's musical community, has always been a place of natural fusions. It lies atop a geological imperfection called the Balcones Fault, which, according to the prevailing lay theories in the area, gives it a peculiar topographical character.

It is the point at which the countryside begins to change dramatically no matter which way you go—quickly evolving into treeless, cattle-producing prairieland as you move north or west, drying up into cactus-covered desert country as you move south towards San Antonio and Mexico, and tangling itself into thick pine woods and murky pockets of swampland as you move east toward Louisiana.

"And," says Murphey, "there is a social and musical analogy. You have the Chicano influence coming up from around San Antonio. You have a lot of blues and even some cajun music spilling over from Louisiana, a pretty large jazz following associated with the university, and north of here country music is incredibly popular. Culturally, you have blacks, Chicanos and a variety of European heritages. And overlaid across all of this, you have the cowboy culture.

"Austin," he concludes, "is the hub. It has a feeling of vitality that's pretty hard to match."

For the past 40 years, there have been people around Austin who felt that way, who appreciated talent for what it was and had the breadth of taste to revel in diversity. Chief among those people in the early years was a kindly old gentleman named Kenneth Threadgill, who transformed a filling station into a beer joint in 1933 and featured live entertainment once a week. Threadgill himself performed with the house band, a hard-country back-up group that blended well with his Jimmie Rodgers style of yodeling.

He also opened his stage to anyone who wanted to play there, and by the time the '60s rolled around, it was an exciting place indeed. One of the people who got her start there was an ex-coed from the University of Texas, a troubled, dynamic young woman named Janis Joplin, who went on to become one of the genuine, hard-living heroines of the West Coast rock culture.

Despite the efforts of people like Threadgill, however, things began to go a little sour in Austin, as they did nearly everywhere else in the late '60s and early '70s. In the wake of Cambodia, Vietnam and Kent and Jackson State, the nation's mood began to darken, and Austin suffered as much as any place. More than some, in fact, for diverse and pluralistic cultures can become a hodge-podge of armed camps if you strip away the veneer of tolerance that prevails in happier times.

One of the people in Austin who understood all this, and had become deeply troubled by it during the early months of the 1970s, was a bearded young lawyer and soft-spoken music buff named Mike Tolleson. Tolleson had become involved with a group of people who had opened a club and community center in August of 1970—a watering hole for freaks called the Armadillo World Headquarters, located in a hollow auditorium a few hundred yards from the Colorado River.

The Armadillo had blossomed out of a search for a congenial place for the struggling, but talented rock musicians who abounded in the Austin area and were resisting the usual migration to the West Coast. Eddie Wilson, manager of a group called Shiva's Headband, had happened to notice one night a vacant auditorium next door to a skating rink, and within a fairly short time he and some friends had transformed it into the Armadillo.

The beat of hard rock soon flourished inside its two-story walls, and the freaks poured in by the droves. The Armadillo people also developed a craft shop and practice room for musicians, and the stature of the place began to grow. But there was a disturbing thought in the back of their minds, a realization that for the most part, only one type of person was apt to come and hear their music; and so they began to experiment a little. Among other things, they brought in the inventor of bluegrass, Bill Monroe, and some country-flavored freak rockers called The Flying Burrito Brothers.

Then, in the summer of 1972, they held their breath and took the biggest plunge yet—a leap back into the hard-core honky-tonking past, with the West Texas beat of Willie Nelson.

"We thought if we could sell Willie to our audience, and bring in his old audience," remembers Mike Tolleson, draping his feet across the corner of his desk, "we could cross sectors and integrate these scenes culturally. That was something we really wanted to do because there had been a real sense of segregation in Austin, a pretty strong feeling of antagonism.

"We thought we could promote a kind of fusion and see different types of people together so that Austin could be a total community. We also brought in Waylon, Tom T. Hall and several others; and what emerged was a pretty different image—people became something more than just hippies, or just rednecks, and it was a very satisfying thing to see it happen."

Few people shared in the satisfaction any more emphatically than Nelson himself. For he is an unusual figure in the country music scene—one of a handful of people (Kris Kristofferson is another) who produces more awe among those who know him well than among those who see him at a distance.

"It's really been an incredible thing," he said recently, thinking back over the past several years, as he crumbled a pair of saltine crackers into a bowl of vegetable soup.

Weary from a week on the road, Nelson had slipped away for a few minutes of conversation in the motel room of his long-time friend and drummer, Paul English. He seemed to savor the reflective minutes before the record company hangers-on and the giggling groupies with their pre-faded jeans and pointy-toed cowboy boots found out where he was and descended like flies.

"Yeah," he continued in the relaxed baritone voice that comes out with a twang when he puts it to music, "it was certainly a good thing. You had all these people who were afraid of each other, or thought they were, though I never quite saw it that way. I had played to enough different kind of crowds to know they had more in common than they thought.

"But it's fun now. You can make a list of all kinds of people that come together at our shows, especially in Texas." He pauses for another slirp at his soup spoon and then continues: "Maybe if we keep putting on the shows, and if the same kind of crowds keep showing up, the time will come when nobody will have to make the lists anymore."

He smiles when he says it, and the smile does not go away altogether when his door bursts open and a record company secretary with a high-pitched voice and jeans that fit like a layer of skin asks if she and her friends can come in. The word has apparently spread, for the room quickly fills up with the faithful, and the serious conversation begins to dissipate.

Nelson is used to it, and he accepts the inevitable with the kind of beatific resignation that has become his trademark. People say the serenity has always been a part of him, though that seems hard to believe if you look back on the early days when there were marriages that fell apart and albums that didn't sell, and when the Music Row producers were telling him he was so good at writing songs, there was really no reason to try and sing them.

Now, of course, everything is different—especially in Texas, where the groupies, freaks, cowboys and old people will travel for hundreds of miles and gather by the tens of thousands just to mingle in his presence. His Fourth of July musical picnics have become a semi-official institution in Texas, with the 1975 outing drawing upwards of 70,000 people.

"Down in Texas," concludes Waylon Jennings in gruff and sincere admiration, "they think that when they die they go to Willie's house."

To some observers, especially the rock-oriented journalists who are not yet hip to the sound of his music, Willie's is a phenomenon that defies explanation. They point out—correctly—that his abilities as a picker, singer and even a songwriter are not markedly more impressive than those of Texas colleagues whose names are less than legend. The question, then, is why Willie?

For starters, there's the fact that fads are contagious, and so is the excitement of a crowd that borders on being a mob. But still, there had to be a beginning point, and people like his drummer, Paul English, believe it's explained at least partially (and maybe even primarily) by the grinning serenity of his presence.

It's hard to say whether that's true, but there was certainly no evidence to the contrary one wintry evening not long ago, when a fairly typical Willie Nelson crowd had assembled in frantic anticipation of his arrival. They endured the warm-up acts, then erupted into routine frenzy when he padded onto the stage with his t-shirt, tennis shoes, and battered Martin guitar.

He began to strum and then realized to his mild embarrassment that his guitar was out of tune. As he began the frustrating twang-twang process of trying to synchronize the strings, he leaned toward the microphone and asked with a grin, "How do you like me so far?" They cheered like maniacs.

Backstage when the show was over, Nelson, like any reasonable person, shied away from talking about auras—realizing that they are not much subject to precise dissection. But if serenity is the key intangible that combines with his music, he will let drop some hints about where he comes from. The hints, he says, are contained in his songs—which certainly seems to be the case.

Most of his tear-jerking jukebox ballads are distinctly autobiographical as are the cuts from an obscure album called "Yesterday's Wine," which came out in 1971, and can now be found in the $2 bins of sophisticated record stores. But if the album didn't sell very well, in Nelson's mind it is nevertheless the most potent and personal record he's ever produced.

It's an opera in a way, a sort of rough country equivalent of "Jesus Christ Superstar"—not so much in its content, but in the originality of its approach. It's a concept album, tracing, with unabashed theological overtones, the ups and downs of a typical life and revealing in the process a crucial fact about Willie Nelson—that despite his honky-tonking history and fast-paced present, he is about as deeply religious as anyone around.

The revelation is scattered throughout the album, but probably is found most clearly in an uncomplicated song called "It's Not For Me To Understand." It's a gospel tune that tells the story of a man walking past a yard full of children, one of whom is a little boy who's blind and standing alone and off to one side. The man, who is Nelson, is moved by the scene and demands to know how God could permit such a heartbreaking turn of events. The answer turns out to be this:

> *After all, you're just a man*
> *And it's not for you to understand*
> *It's not for you to reason why*
> *You too are blind without my eyes.*

It's a frankly sentimental song, but the humility it contains is the profound and cosmic variety that comes, Nelson says, when religion sinks in deep. And it can provide, he adds, some pretty stout emotional armor against the vagaries and absurdities of everyday life.

In any event, Nelson's eventual stardom has proven an understandable inspiration to a host of Texas pickers whose day has not yet arrived. And so he became the catalyst. The momentum began to grow, and almost overnight, Austin filled up with a remarkably talented array of poets and musicians of every stripe.

The supply had been around for some time in the form of people like Rusty Weir, but the legions were beefed up considerably in the early '70s when Jerry Jeff Walker, Michael Murphey, Steve Fromholz, Doug Sahm, Townes Van Zandt and quite a few others moved in to stay.

Of all of those, one of the most significant has turned out to be

Sahm, who made it pretty big in the mid to late '60s as the lead singer for a British-style rock group called the Sir Douglas Quintet. What the teeny-boppers didn't know, however, and probably didn't want to know, was that Sahm and the quintet were products of the very un-English city of San Antonio, Texas.

He had grown up there in the '40s and '50s—a fiddle-playing prodigy in the redneck honky-tonks, who also had a habit of wandering crosstown to the blues clubs, to share a stage with the likes of T-Bone Walker. But it was rock 'n' roll that finally took hold of Sahm's life during the high school years, and after graduation he gathered together a quintet of rockers and headed for the coast.

There was a string of mid-'60s hits, including "She's About A Mover" and "Mendicino." But things grew quieter after that, until Sahm resurfaced in 1972 with a slap-happy solo album featuring a whole bunch of country songs, and some able back-up work by a musical compatriot named Bob Dylan.

Sahm had moved back to Texas by that time, settling in comfortably on the rock side of the country-rock spectrum, and he has been there ever since. He lives now in a cabin on the outskirts of Austin, nestled in among the scrub oaks a few hundred yards from a music hall hangout called the Soap Creek saloon.

He agrees with little hesitation these days to talk about his musical odyssey (he prefers to call it a trip), but with an eye for privacy, he generally suggests the club, rather than the cabin, as the site for discussion. It is probably a better choice on a number of counts, for the Soap Creek is a delightful place, congenial and easy-going with low ceilings, pool tables and an adjacent 300-seat concert room with a double-size fireplace.

The interview is set for late afternoon, and the club is inhabited only by a waitress and a couple of good ole boys who have been there long enough for the Lone Star beer to give way to a round of Tequila Sunrises. Against the wall, an early vintage Wurlitzer juke box is standing idle, but next to it a more modern version loaded with Doug Sahm records is blaring forth with "Groover's Paradise," the title cut from his latest album.

The man himself strolls in after a few minutes—looking for all the world like the ageless Mr. Hippie. He's 34 years old, but there's absolutely no way to tell with his T-shirt uniform, angular face, and shoulder-length hair, which is straight and getting on toward being unkempt.

He plops his slender frame into a chair near the bar, and offers to let a pair of eastern visitors finish their game of eight-ball before the conversation gets underway. But he seems obviously antsy and ready to get on with it, so the cue sticks are temporarily laid to rest and the pitcher of Lone Star is transported to the center of his table.

It soon becomes apparent that interviewing Sahm without a tape recorder is a mistake. Asking a question is like flicking a switch and the ideas spew out like champagne from a shook-up bottle—the syntax askew, the transitions non-existent, but somewhere in there a nugget of understanding that holds your attention.

For example, there was a point early in the conversation when he was asked what brought him back to Austin. The answer came out something like this:

"Well, I was out there on that whole West Coast scene, man, you know, in San Francisco, that whole Grateful Dead trip, you know; it was getting pretty heavy, I don't know, it just kinda burned itself out . . . you know what I mean, like big cities, like what's happening in New York today, you know, so I just came back to Austin, well first to San Antonio, which is where I grew up, but then here in '72. I can't 'splain it; probably Charlotte is the same way, or Macon, you know? I mean they didn't just burn out, people are still there, there are still jobs; and we got into the country thing, and our music now is countrier than ever. I can't 'splain it."

Or words to that effect.

The odd thing is that after awhile, it all seems to make sense, and the following themes begin to crystallize: that in his mind, the big city scene has basically turned bad; that there is some kind of analogy or connection between the bummed-out craziness of the Haight-Ashbury drug culture, the proliferating concrete of urban Los Angeles, and the teetering financial problems of New York City. In the face of those things, Sahm believes, a lot of people are heading back to less complicated places, and more specifically, in many cases they are heading home—back to the roots.

And that reality, he says, is one of the key energizing forces of the Austin musical movement.

Sahm runs through all of that, and once he has explained it to his satisfaction if not everyone else's, he sniffs and belches, slaps both hands on his thighs, and says abruptly: "Well, is that about it?" It turns out that it is, and he arises, shakes hands and reaffirms his earlier declaration that he wants to "do some gigs" back east in places like North Carolina.

Behind him a waitress with a friendly smile and a Doug Sahm T-shirt, which she fills out impressively, shakes her head in the perpetual amazement that Sahm seems to generate. "He's something else, isn't he?" she says with a laugh, and then launches into a monologue on the crowds that pour into the Soap Creek when Sir Doug performs.

"It's really weird," she says. "You get a little bit of everybody here. For a long time, it was a young, kinda freaky crowd. The older folks were a little scared of the place. The first year or so, there were some people who came out here that were into dealing drugs, but we've got that cleared up, and now it's a real mixture. The freaky ones still come, but so do some older, you know, straighter people. And there are a lot of people like in their 20s—late 20s—and 30s."

That in-between crowd is hard to define. They are not exactly freaks, and they don't look like rednecks, and in fact, they seem to include a little bit of everybody.

Some, for example, are 30ish, one-time collegiate radicals whose lives have mirrored, in a kind of political way, the musical gyrations of Sahm. They grew up as un-selfconscious conservatives in places like Dallas or the dust-bowl towns farther west, then went away to school and found themselves permanently radicalized and temporarily alienated by the war and the upheavals of the past 10 years.

They may have no more intention of giving up their politics than Sahm has of backing away entirely from rock 'n' roll. But if you talk to people like Rick Ream and Pamela Owens, a young Texas couple who had settled in recently at one of the country music clubs in downtown Austin, they will tell you they are fed up with the alienation and have come back to Texas because it's home.

That is a part of the crowd, but there are also others. There are the rednecks and good ole boys who are young enough to have been influenced by the turmoil of recent decades—not only the war, but the ethnic awakenings and the mind-numbing string of cultural fads from Beatlemania to the present. Their hair may be a little bit longer, and their ideas a little bit different from what they used to be. But they are, as an up-and-coming singer named Milton Carroll put it, "your basic country audience."

"It's really a hell of a thing, man," says Carroll, whose first album has just come out on Willie Nelson's Lone Star label. "It's roots, you know what I mean? There ain't no way to change where you're from."

And if you can't change it, you may as well flaunt it, and they do a lot of that at places like the Castle Creek Club in downtown Austin. When Friday night rolls around, they will pour from the woodwork with their cowboy hats and faded denims—clapping and swaying and whooping like crazy people, while up on the stage Jerry Jeff Walker is blitzed as usual and leading a cast of his buddies through "Goodnight Irene" and "Will The Circle Be Unbroken?"

The applause and rebel yells will sometimes linger for a full five minutes after he is through, and he will return to the microphone, lurching forward with a grin and say, "These are hongry people. They'll clap for anything."

But those scenes are not limited to Texas. Roughly the same thing happened, for example, in Charlotte's Park Center a few months back, and it's a peculiar sight in a part of the country where the nearest real cowboy is a thousand miles away.

There are excesses in there someplace, and they can be disturbing to the grizzled Texans whose identity has never been much in doubt, and who are a little put off at the prospect of having their culture turned into something it isn't. And indeed if the dusty boots trappings were all there were to it, the Austin Sound would no doubt melt into the past as quickly as hula hoops, bomb shelters and blue suede shoes.

But after five years, it shows no signs of melting and in fact is growing in popularity. And the reason for that, of course, is that there is more to it. Beneath the shit-kicking exterior, there is a celebration of the humaneness that has always resided in the Texas culture, and nowhere is that fact illustrated more graphically than in the music of Guy Clark.

Clark is a decent, Sleepy-John type of fellow, who grew up in the western flatlands town of Monahans, then wound up in Nashville a few years back with a promising contract to write some songs. Although he no longer lives in Texas, he still performs there and writes from his boyhood there—from the days during World War II and afterward, when he was raised by an oil-drilling drifter named Jack Prigg.

Prigg was, as Clark puts it, "my grandmother's boyfriend," a tobacco-chewing, domino-playing old man, whose life and death and friendship heightened in Clark an instinctive understanding that you find in the most poetic song-writers—a realization that there are generally human and hopeful qualities in even the saddest and most tawdry of circumstances. Thus, Clark has, in the course of his 34 years, genuinely befriended all sorts of people, from winos, to hitchhikers, to prostitutes, and his music as a result is shot through with a kind of rough-hewn sympathy and sensitivity.

Probably the best example of all that is the song he wrote about Prigg, which goes, in part, like so:

I'd play the Red River Valley
And he'd sit in the kitchen and cry
And run his fingers through 70 years of livin'
And wonder Lord, has every well I drilled run dry
We was friends me and this old man
Like desperados waiting for a train . . .

He's a drifter and a driller of oil wells
And an old school man of the world
He taught me how to drive his car when he's too drunk to
And he'd wink and give me money for the girls
And our lives was like some old western movie
Like desperados waiting for the train . . .

The day before he died I went to see him
I was grown and he was almost gone
So we just closed our eyes and dreamed us up a kitchen
And sang another verse of that old song
Come on Jack, that son of a bitch is coming
And we're desperados waiting for the train . . .

—Sunbury Music
Copyright 1973

Although the scenery of the song is taken from Texas, the feelings behind it are too universal to be confined to a region. The same is true of much of the other music coming out of Austin, and as a result the fans are multiplying throughout the country.

A lot of them are young, like the 5,000 or so Vanderbilt University students who turned out for Clark and Willie Nelson not long ago and grabbed hold of country music like it had been invented especially for them. There were people around Nashville who grumbled after that that Willie had turned his back on country music's traditional fans, and Roy Acuff even said as much on the stage of the Grand Ole Opry.

But the theory came tumbling down a few weeks later when Nelson was invited to appear at the Midnight Jamboree at Ernest Tubb's Record Shop. It was a performance, as it turned out, that underscored as clearly as any other the symbolism of the Texas movement.

For Ernest Tubb's is a funky place. Its Midnight Jamborees every Saturday night now draw the stalwarts who have never quite adjusted to the fact that the Grand Ole Opry had gone uptown and moved to a new location. They are the hard-core folk who still pour in from the hinterlands in their pick-ups and workday khakis to revel in the music of white man's soul.

But when Nelson appeared back in mid-October, the crowd was a little bit different. It contained, in addition to its regulars, a smattering of Nelson's newer and shaggier fans, and there were discreet murmurs in various parts of the room about why the hippies were there. Some of the murmurs, in fact, were directed toward Nelson himself, who arrived late and had to make his way through the throngs with his flaming red beard and a blue-checkered bandana looped around his shoulder-length hair.

But when he finally got to the stage and began to sing, the mood changed abruptly and they whooped and screamed and wouldn't let him leave. And in the back of the crowd, the whole event was summed up pretty eloquently by an ole boy with close cropped hair and a round, perpetually flushed face.

"Yep," he said, rocking back and forth from heel to toe, as his voice took on an air of authority. "Ole Willie'll be all right."

CHAPTER 9

The Other Side of Southern Justice

Although many of the passages affecting the South and the nation have been reflected in music, the political manifestations, it seems to me, are still the most concrete and crucial. With that in mind, I participated in an award-winning Charlotte Observer series on the 25th anniversary of the Supreme Court's Brown decision—an extremely important ruling, which struck down the segregation of schools and herald-ed a period of judicial activism.

My part of the series was mainly historical—to trace the origins and evolution of an important judicial saga, to see how precedents established in Deep South court-rooms affected the nation as a whole. I was impressed by the ironies surrounding federal judges in the South. They struck me as real-life Atticus Finches—men who never sought controversy, but who simply planted their feet, behaving with a certain grace, stubbornness and aristocratic certainty.

Parts of this story have been told earlier in the book, chiefly in chapter two. But that was the black man's side of the drama. What follows is an often overlooked seg-ment of the white man's response—the legacy of a handful of highly principled Southerners who, for more than 20 years, exercised enormous sway in the affairs of the country The legacy, however, is beginning to fade.

March, 1979

There is a tiny brass plaque at 61 Meeting St. in Charleston, S.C., a tarnished reminder that the house is old—a certified piece of tradition in a neighborhood dating to the 17th century. But the plaque says nothing about the man who lived in the house, which seems an odd and deliberate oversight.

Charleston is famous for the homage it pays to aristocratic heroes—to secessionists, Civil War generals, and warriors of the American Revolution. But there is a crucial difference between the rebellions of Francis Marion or John C. Calhoun, and the more recent heresies of Judge J. Waties Waring.

There is a comfortable quality about revolutions that have faded in-to history. The violence and the sense of upheaval are absorbed and gentled by the passage of time.

And so it is that chiseled stone monuments—shrouded by wisteria vines and twisting live oak branches—still honor the rhetoric of secession. Antebellum cannons still aim their malevolence across the Charleston Harbor, pointing to the spot where the Civil War began. But the legal and social revolution that gained momentum (some would even say it started) in the somber, pine-paneled courtroom of Judge Waring is the object of official neglect. Its effects are to unsettling, too much a part of today, to permit much homage.

Waring became, in his 61st year, a U.S. District Judge—the first in America to hear an overt challenge to the segregation of schools or to hand down a pair of sweeping, bluntly worded rulings giving black people the right to vote.

It was not a role that he sought or expected to play. For the first six decades of his life, he was a pillar of Charleston's tranquility—an aristocratic lawyer and mildly ambitious politician, who belonged to all the right clubs, believed all the right things, and was honored and admired by his fellow Charlestonians.

Like so many of his colleagues in the federal judiciary, he had achieved his lofty position precisely because he never rocked any boats. But he came to the bench in the 1940s—the beginning of a period of judicial history that was one of the most wrenching the country had ever known.

Federal judges, particularly in the South, were compelled to deal over the next 30 years with a bewildering array of constitutional issues—from voting rights to school segregation, from police brutality to the future of nuclear energy. Because of rulings by Southern judges—precedents set in Deep South courtrooms—cities from Boston to Los Angeles have wrestled with busing and school integration for the better part of a decade.

A whole race has been given access to the ballot, mental patients have been guaranteed the right to treatment, and legislatures across the country have been reapportioned—shifting the balance of political power from rural America to the nation's cities.

For all of that, the judges themselves have paid a price. If their rulings often tore at the domestic tranquility of their region and nation, there have been similar effects on the comfortable, uneventful lives that most of them had known.

"Federal judges," concludes Robert Merhige, a district judge in Richmond, Va., "don't start lawsuits. But the cases began, and they started coming to all of us. That's what the federal courts are for. They are places where minorities can come, where they ought to come. In the South, of course, that often meant blacks, and the racial issue was probably the most unsettling we had to deal with. Because of the laws we had in our region, the attack on legal segregation—especially segregated schools—began in the South."

More precisely, you could argue, the attack began on a dusty backroad in Clarendon County, S.C., in a creaky, paint-chipped cabin belonging to Harry Briggs. They met one night in 1948—a half dozen black men, frightened at the potential consequences of their rebellion, but knowing in the end there was no turning back.

Their concern was schools—the gaping disparity between the facilities and opportunities afforded to Clarendon County's white children, and those afforded their own. The county, in those days, was one of the state's most primitive—a swatch of picked over cotton fields and murky, black-water swamplands that yielded a meager and reluctant living to the people who clung to the land. And overlaid against all of that was the specter of segregation.

"It seems almost unbelievable when you look back at it," affirms Billie S. Fleming, a longtime leader in the Clarendon NAACP, a large and genial man who exudes the dignity and assurance his people were striving for in the 1940s.

"I remember when I was a boy, coming through schools in the '20s and '30s, almost all the money went for white schools. Blacks got only what was left over—and that was nothing but some money to pay a few teachers. The state and county did not provide us with bricks and mortar, and when we built facilities for ourselves, the county didn't even furnish fuel and utilities. Public-spirited citizens would chop wood and haul it on wagons so the children could have some heat.

"In the majority of cases, there was only one teacher per school, usually teaching six or eight grades. Public transportation was provided only for white students, even when blacks lived 10 or 12 miles from a high school. It seems unbelievable," he concludes with a tug at his graying mustache. "But that's how it was."

Conditions had changed very little by the 1940s, and in response, Clarendon's black people decided to take their concerns to federal court—to Judge Waring, who was rapidly emerging as a man with a sympathetic ear.

When they first arrived in Waring's court, the Clarendon plaintiffs weren't asking for anything radical. They simply wanted decent and equalized facilities—such basic amenities as indoor plumbing and heated buildings on cold winter mornings. But when the dust finally settled, they had, at Waring's urging, redrawn their suit—demanding nothing less than the total dismantling of a segregated school system.

The decision to pursue such a drastic course did not come easily. It became intertwined with the national policies of the NAACP, which had entered the Clarendon case at the request of the Rev. J. A. DeLaine and the county's other black leaders.

The NAACP's chief strategist in those days was a tough and aggressive attorney named Thurgood Marshall, later a justice on the U.S. Supreme Court. He had long understood the pitfalls of an outright attack on segregation itself—the potential for disaster if such an all-or-nothing course were to fall flat on its face.

He knew that in 1896, the Supreme Court had handed down its Plessy v. Ferguson ruling—affirming the constitutionality of separate but equal facilities for blacks and whites. Throughout the 1940s, the NAACP's primary strategy was to seek an implementation of the Plessy precedent—to file a series of lawsuits charging that while schools for black and white were officially separate, they were also decidedly unequal.

The strategy was proving effective in cases throughout the South, most of them higher education suits in Texas, Louisiana and North Carolina. Gradually, Marshall and his fellow attorneys were chipping away at the problem, dramatizing the hypocrisy of separate but equal, and securing a steady stream of rulings requiring better black schools.

The attorneys knew that the cost of providing segregated—but truly equal—public schools systems would prove to be exorbitant. Eventually, they hoped, the South would find the price too high.

Marshall, however, was consistently uncomfortable with such a gradual and circuitous approach to breaking down the walls of segregation. He began to declare in his public speeches that the NAACP was committed to a reversal of the Plessy precedent, to a ringing affirmation by the U.S. Supreme Court that separate was inherently unequal.

As it happened, his public declarations coincided with the NAACP's entry into the Clarendon County case—a fact that Marshall found disturbing. He couldn't imagine a worse test case for total integration, since Clarendon was a poor, rural and majority black county with a history of racial hostility.

He knew that if he abandoned his strategy of the past, he would be asking not only for the radical, unheard-of step of integrating public schools, but also for the busing of whites into a minority situation. He decided to hedge his bets, arguing in passing that separate could never be equal, but emphasizing that in any case, Clarendon's black schools should be drastically improved.

Fleming remembers the response of Judge Waring, how he peered from the bench with a somber expression on his round, friendly face. He summoned Marshall forward, and then, according to Fleming, "He told us, 'you're going down the wrong road. If you really want the courts to declare segregation to be unconstitutional, you need to draw your arguments exactly that way.' "

Marshall and the blacks of Clarendon County would have been dumbfounded by such advice from a Deep South judge if they had not watched the gradual transformation of Waring from the time he was appointed to the bench.

Born in 1880, the judge was raised in a time when Reconstruction had taken a firm hold of South Carolina. His was a genteel lineage, running back through eight generations of Charlestonians, and while he was never an out-and-out race-baiter, neither did he question the social order of the day. "Most of the Negroes I knew were ex-slaves," he would later recall. "You loved them and were good to them. We didn't give them any rights, but they never asked for any rights, and I didn't question it. I was raised in the atmosphere that we ought to take care of these people."

Waring's noblesse oblige sensibilities were deeply offended early in his tenure on the bench. It began with a peonage dispute, a case in which a white man was accused of detaining a black and forcing him to work for almost nothing. Waring ordered the white man to jail. Later, he would order South Carolina's Democratic Party to allow blacks to vote in statewide primaries and would require equal salaries for the state's black and white teachers.

His life, at that point, began to change. Hate mail poured into his office. Late night telephone calls brought threats and promises of bodily harm. And one October evening in 1950, three pistol shots rang through the Charleston night—the ricochet narrowly missing Waring and his wife, Elizabeth, as they played canasta in the living room.

But at least as unsettling as the threats were the more sophisticated retributions of Waring's fellow bluebloods. During more tranquil times, when he was Charleston's city attorney, he would step out his front door and stroll briskly past the swaying palms of Meeting Street, smiling, waving and chatting with friends during his one-block walk to city hall.

Such strolls soon became lonely. Party invitations, once numerous, dried up entirely, and even Waring's own family reacted as if a leper had appeared in its midst. The change was sealed by his role in the school case, and at age 70, Waring found his life transformed—found himself wholly alienated from the people and values of his first 60 years.

It did not help—in fact the situation became more nasty—when the Supreme Court affirmed Waring's view that segregation was unconstitutional, declaring in 1954, and in a follow-up ruling in 1955, that America's schools must be desegregated with all deliberate speed.

Following the high court's sweeping proclamation (which was based on the Clarendon case and four others, including Brown v. Topeka, Kan.), Waring resigned his judgeship and moved to New York to spend his remaining years. He had been sustained in Charleston only by his wife and a few black friends, and the loneliness eventually took its toll.

It was a peculiar, and in some ways tragic, scene in 1968 when Waring returned to Charleston for the final time—to be buried in one of the city's oldest cemeteries, lowered to earth in a plain pine casket. A handful of whites—his wife, a minister and an efficient-looking undertaker—watched in silence, while behind them nearly 300 blacks lowered their heads in a final gesture of respect.

Many of them were from Clarendon County, and like the judge, they too had felt the sting of retribution—at times had felt it even more acutely, as the white man's counterattack cost them homes, farms and the ability to make a living. But it was a price they paid in behalf of themselves, and never had they seen a white man willing to match their sacrifice.

"I remember one time the judge and I were talking," recalls Fleming. "He was always a gentleman, never bitter about the things he went through, and one day he asked in his quiet way. He said, 'Mr. Fleming, do you really believe that I have helped your people?' I said, 'Yes sir, Judge, I do. More than any man since Abraham Lincoln.' "

The same year Waring was buried, an equally unimposing, unthreatening man was taking the oath of office 200 miles away in Charlotte. James McMillan, a respected lawyer who grew up in the flat, tobacco country farmlands of Robeson County, N.C., knew from the beginning that a federal judgeship had its pitfalls. He was aware of the examples, not only of Waring, but of dozens of others around the South—particularly Frank Johnson, a stubborn, independent Republican from the hills of northern Alabama.

Johnson was appointed to the bench in 1956, and since that time he had been called upon to decide the legality of nearly every conceivable aspect of Alabama society. He had desegregated buses, bus terminals, jails and prisons, museums, mental institutions and more than 100 school systems in his district.

But controversy came in other forms as well. He declared that Alabama's mental institutions had a responsibility to treat, as well as confine, their inmates and ordered them emptied if they didn't attempt to do it. He abolished the Alabama poll tax and ordered the reapportionment of the state legislature—following the one-man, one-vote precedent established by his fellow Southern Republican, Judge William Miller of Nashville.

For those things, of course, Johnson paid a price. His former classmate at the University of Alabama, Gov. George Wallace, declared him political enemy number one. Death threats were common, and Johnson was shunned by proper Montgomery society just as Waring was in Charleston.

McMillan was aware that similar consequences could come his way, but he didn't dwell on the prospect. He is not a man with a martyr

Judge McMillan, 1977

complex, and he certainly didn't expect hard times and bitterness to descend in the form that they eventually took.

But in 1968, a group of Charlotte blacks, represented by civil rights lawyer Julius Chambers, re-opened the local school desegregation suit, contending progress to that point had been minimal at best. McMillan was unsympathetic at first. But Chambers' carefully prepared case turned him around, and he issued, in 1969, perhaps the most stunning school desegregation ruling in the history of the country.

He ordered the Charlotte-Mecklenburg school system to use "any and all known ways of desegregation, including busing" to completely desegregate the schools by the fall of 1970. And when the U.S. Supreme Court unanimously sustained him in 1971, it raised the possibility of meaningful—that is, total—school integration nearly anywhere in America.

Not long ago, McMillan parked himself behind a table in a Charlotte restaurant and offered a wistful and typically low-keyed assessment of his role in Swann v. Charlotte-Mecklenburg schools.

"Legally speaking," he explained in his muted Carolina accents, "I've had a number of cases that were considerably more challenging. The Swann case was simply a matter of absorbing the education and then working up the courage to act on what I absorbed. It took me a little while to do it."

It was, as usual, a brief and understated monologue. And McMillan—never very expansive when the conversation centers on himself—found his train of thought continually disrupted by people passing his table and paying their respects. Though he didn't say so, the disruptions had to contain a certain measure of ironic satisfaction, for there was a time only a few years ago when such pleasantries would have been a rare occurrence indeed.

When the community began to grasp that his ruling was for real, McMillan was hanged in effigy. There were demonstrations at his modest brick home near the Charlotte Country Club, and death threats became an accepted part of his life.

McMillan doesn't like to talk about such things today, and even at the time, he retained a remarkable level of dignity and calmness. He has a Presbyterian's fatalism—a sense, as he puts it, that "God has a plan for our lives, and we're a lot better off if we can try not to fight it."

He also discerned, in a short time, some heartening signs that Charlotte was adjusting to the change. In 1975, an ad hoc citizens group, working with the school system's staff, devised what McMillan considered a fair and stable desegregation plan, and the judge closed the case as an active piece of litigation.

He praised his fellow Charlotteans for their maturity and restraint and announced he was "retiring from the education business." But if

Anti-busing protesters parade in
front of Judge McMillan's house, 1970.

McMillan held doggedly to his perspective and good humor during his own personal ordeal, he was deeply disturbed by other judicial developments during the same period.

By the mid '70s, he believes, there had been a major alteration in the rules of the game—of the Supreme Court precedents that govern his job. It bothers him, for deep down, McMillan believes in the march of judicial and social history that began in the courtroom of J. Waties Waring. And so it was with a deep sense of gloom that he watched it all end—in the illustrious, one-time Civil War capital of Richmond, Va.

Above the mantel in the homey judicial chambers of Judge Robert Merhige, there hangs a large and gilded portrait of a famous Virginian. His light brown hair is long and flowing; his steady eyes are gazing toward a window and beyond it the stately form of the Virginia state capitol.

It has been 170 years since the man in the portrait, Chief Justice John Marshall of the fledgling U.S. Supreme Court, walked up the steps of that very building to convene one of the most historic trials his young republic had ever known. The defendant was a former vice president by the name of Aaron Burr—a man accused of plotting and leading a violent attempt to overthrow his government. As part of his defense, Burr asked the court to subpoena his chief accuser, President Thomas Jefferson.

After much soul-searching, Marshall decided to grant Burr's request—an act of judicial impudence that helped transform the federal courts, making them, for the first time, a coequal branch of government with Congress and the President. Rarely has that transformation—the legacy and prestige flowing from the muscle flexing of Justice Marshall—been as important as it has in the past 25 years.

Throughout the '50s, '60s and early '70s, the U.S. Supreme Court was a critical, sustaining force for the district judges on the Deep South firing line. In some cases, it was out in front of them, pulling them reluctantly down a path of judicial and social change. At the very least it was behind them, providing support.

But Chief Justice Earl Warren, a Dwight Eisenhower Republican who had gradually emerged as a hated figure to America's conservatives, resigned in 1969 and was replaced by a man named Warren Earl Burger. Almost everyone, from President Richard Nixon on down, expected a different philosophy from the Burger court. It took a while for the philosophy to jell (it was Burger, after all, who wrote the opinion sustaining the busing decree of James McMillan.) But eventually, Nixon and the others proved correct in their expectations, and one of the earliest, most definitive indicators came at the expense of the man who presides in John Marshall's old courtroom, Judge Robert Merhige of Richmond.

At about the same time that the Supreme Court affirmed McMillan's ruling on busing, Merhige was carrying the logic a step further. He ruled in a case affecting Richmond city schools, and those of surrounding suburban school systems, that busing across school district lines was a permissible tool to achieve integration.

News of the decision was received with alarm in the big cities of the North—in places like Boston, Detroit and Indianapolis, where inner city schools were carefully set apart from predominantly white suburban systems that wanted no part of total integration. Court-watchers and proponents of desegregation knew that in many cases, northern integration would hinge on the Supreme Court's response to the Merhige ruling.

Merhige thought he was on firm legal ground for a number of reasons. For one thing, he had handled more than 40 school desegregation suits, and it seemed a short and easy step from his earlier rulings to the conclusion he reached in the Richmond case—that if the existence of suburban school systems, with their heavy white ratios, made it impossible to integrate the whole Richmond area, then busing between the suburbs and the city was a necessary step.

The judge was surprised, perhaps even stung, when the Supreme Court rejected his logic in 1972. Among his peers, Merhige is widely regarded as a fair-minded jurist, who rarely suffers reversal by a higher court. It's logical that it would be that way, for despite a layman's reputation for judicial activism—for aggressive and sometimes unsettling rulings on everything from integration to prison reform—Merhige brings a conservative, almost civics-teacher definition to the nature of his work.

"My job," he says simply, "is to interpret the Constitution the way the Supreme Court says it should be interpreted. Whether I personally agree or disagree is of absolutely no consequence."

The more you talk to him, the more genuine the humility seems to be, and the more it appears to spring from a deep fascination with history. Merhige has spent more than his share of hours pacing and pondering beneath John Marshall's gold-framed portrait. He is sometimes overwhelmed by the power of the legacy. And yet, in his times of trial, it has also sustained him—has left him with a sense of the past that provides perspective on his own ordeals.

Sitting behind his cluttered wooden desk, glasses perched precariously on the end of his nose, Merhige reflected recently about his years on the bench. He had been, before his appointment in 1967, a hard-working trial lawyer—a transplanted Yankee with a thriving practice and a passion for his work.

It was a safe and lucrative occupation compared to his current calling, but Merhige seems to have had few regrets—even during the raging controversies that left him a household name in Richmond, sometimes hated, sometimes grudgingly admired, but a man who is known to almost everyone.

The notoriety came quickly. He had been on the bench for less than two weeks when black revolutionary H. Rap Brown was arrested in Virginia on a firearms charge and came before Merhige seeking release until his trial. Merhige let him go.

"There was a big hullabaloo about it," the judge recalled. "It was the first time I had given any thought to public reaction. There were pickets around the courthouse, some kooky calls, but that's all part of it."

As the controversies continued to pile on top of each other, so did the vehemence of the public reaction. But Merhige hung in with a feisty, low-keyed tenacity. He refused to acquire an unlisted phone number, despite the hate-spewing calls that came late at night. And one day in a restaurant, when a matronly Virginian called him a son-of-a-bitch and spat in his face, he simply wiped away the damage with a handkerchief and walked away.

Later, he would bring the same kind of stubborn resignation to his Supreme Court reversal. "It so happens I agreed with the rulings we were handing down," he explains quietly. "But that, I don't think, is of any consequence. The law is what the Supreme Court says it is, and whatever labels you put on the court—conservative, liberal—it changes. But that's what brings balance."

Merhige paused for a moment, absently flicking a ball point pen, as his deeply rooted Catholicism and his almost mystical view of the American system intertwined themselves in his mind. "I thank God we had the courts," he continued. "They are not places where pleasant things happen, but they are the final peaceful forum in this country.

"I think," he concluded finally, "that God has a very special view of America. Lord knows if he didn't, we would have made a pretty big mess of it ourselves. And all of these changes, I'm satisfied, are for the good."

Good or bad, the changes have been dramatic and have come in a clump. In the five years following its reversal of Merhige, the Supreme Court handed down rulings approving capital punishment, allowing teachers to spank their students, making it harder for minorities to bring class action lawsuits, and permitting the use of property taxes to finance education—even when the results are unequal, underfunded schools for low-income children.

If Merhige brings a long-run, blind-faith optimism to those kinds of trends, his Charlotte colleague and admirer, James McMillan, does not. "A lower court judge," McMillan says bluntly, "is bound by higher court decisions. But he is not bound to keep his mouth shut on the wisdom of those decisions."

And McMillan does not, in fact, keep his mouth shut.

In his soft-spoken way, he has publicly chastised his fellow jurists—usually in speeches at various legal conventions. The thing that troubles him most, he says, is the growing tendency of some judges (including those on the Supreme Court) to dodge the basic issues of a case through the use of legal technicalities.

McMillan felt the result of that tendency in 1976 in the most recent landmark case to come his way—a complicated suit that temporarily clouded the future of the nuclear power industry.

Legally, the primary issue was the constitutionality of the Price-Anderson Act, a 20-year-old law that limited the liability of power companies in the case of a nuclear disaster. Duke Power Co., the defendant in the suit, argued that the act was an essential piece of protection—that without it, power companies would lose necessary investors and might find themselves unable to operate nuclear plants.

The company also argued that the chances of a nuclear disaster were extremely remote—an argument McMillan rejected in a ruling that declared the Price-Anderson law unconstitutional. "The court is not a bookie," he wrote. "The significant conclusion is that, under the odds quoted by either side, a nuclear catastrophe is a real, not fanciful, possibility."

Despite the sweeping implications of the case, most of the legal maneuvering centered on an issue that was far more trivial. "The most seriously litigated point," McMillan later recalled with a shrug of frustration, "was not the constitutional issue that was being raised, but Duke Power's contention that under recent Supreme Court precedents, the plaintiffs had no right to be in court."

Eventually, the Supreme Court ruled with Duke, adding to McMillan's frustration. He believes that federal courts must be accessible to almost anyone—that legal fees alone make it hard for most people to get there, and that the Burger court's attempts to add to the difficulty are a stab at the heart of democracy.

McMillan holds that view even though his own district has dispensed with more than 1,700 cases—an average of at least three a day— in the past two years, leaving him wobbly under the load. But the answer, he thinks, is more judges, rather than fewer cases or the dodging of complicated issues.

"It seems clear to me," he concluded recently at the end of a hearty lunch, "that a judge's first duty is to decide the primary issues of a case for the people who have brought it to court."

He paused and fell silent after that, pondering what to him is an unhappy fact: that America's courts—and therefore the U.S. Constitution—are no longer the instruments he believes they should be, and that the judicial legacy of J. Waties Waring has slowly begun to fade.

CHAPTER 10

A Final Tribute
to Raymond Wheeler

Sometimes if you are a white Southerner, and if you are inclined to be critical of the sins of your heritage, it is hard to find heroes. One of mine was Raymond Wheeler. His sensibilities were not unlike those of the Southern federal judges in the preceeding chapter. But Raymond was a doctor. He was a brilliant man, who saw the connection between the illness he combatted in the course of his practice and the larger social ills that, for many Southerners, made good health impossible.

Raymond died suddenly in 1982, and I was called in to write his obituary. This is it. I include it here despite certain lapses in journalistic quality and distance. It offers an opportunity for people to remember him, and for those who didn't know him to catch a glimpse of his life.

February, 1982

First, they are shocked and numb and their admiration overflows, and they begin to talk in run-away superlatives. They talk about his compassion, sensitivity and dedication to causes—his peculiar ego that required little feeding. But then some of them will pause at a curious realization, chuckling perhaps in the midst of their grief at how Raymond Wheeler himself would respond to their words.

His friends know that he would squirm and change the subject—perhaps with a certain diffidence, an aloofness and reserve that lent an odd coolness to the outrage at his core. Then some of them will talk about that outrage—how Wheeler, a Charlotte physician and civil rights advocate who died Wednesday night, would tour Mississippi during the steamy summers of the '60s, recording his shock at the conditions that he found.

His findings led to a prime-time CBS documentary called "Hunger in America"—and also to his own stormy testimonials before assorted committees of Congress, when he would fortify himself with a lunchtime martini and assail the sensibilities of indifferent Southern senators. He could be eloquent on those occasions, or in his frequent public speeches amidst the violence of the times. Sometimes he seemed to

teeter on the edge of some despair, hoping for the best, but recognizing also that the worst was very possible.

"And now there are new leaders," he told the Southern Regional Council, a biracial civil rights organization that he headed in 1967, "determined to give us no choice but to hear a different message. They are saying that they no longer have any faith in the expressed good intentions of white America, that the existence of the black people today is intolerable. . . . And if America should choose the course of violent reaction, if it should be so foolish as to attempt to seal the ghettos with guns and soldiers—hoping the problem will go away—then these young men are saying they will make it as hard on us as possible. And the wreckage will be the wreckage and ashes, not just of our cities but of the American dream."

Such phrases seem faintly dated in the quieter times of the early 1980s. But in the 1960s they were startling declarations—affronts to many of Wheeler's fellow Southerners.

Many people, however, remember him differently from that—not as an orator, but as a shy and smallish man of 62, a lover of good jokes who was unable to tell them, a graying physician with a certain sadness about him, who still made house calls with his fading black bag.

"His instincts were terribly good," said his medical partner, Dr. William Porter. "He would stand there and look and listen for a while—just sort of tune in when the patient came in. He not only understood the science of medicine, he had the art to underpin it. His powers of observation were as acute in the examining room as they were in the midst of the shanties of Mississippi."

Wheeler grew up in rural North Carolina, in the Pitt County community of Farmville in the eastern part of the state. He escaped to the University of North Carolina near the end of the Depression, got his medical degree from Washington University in St. Louis in 1943, then fought in World War II at the Battle of the Bulge. He never talked much about his wartime adventures, except to tell one friend who proposed a camping trip that he promised himself on his return home from Germany never to sleep on the ground when a bed was available.

From the beginning, somehow, he was caught up in civil rights—seeing the connection between the illness he encountered in the course of his profession and the horrifying conditions in which some Americans lived.

"He sort of carried a constant sense of outrage," said Kathryn Waller, director of the Charlotte-based Rural Advancement Fund, which Wheeler helped found. "It was an outrage over people not having—in our affluent, free society—the basics to survive."

As Mrs. Waller will attest, however, Wheeler was impatient with mere rhetoric on the subject—viewing it as too easy and ultimately ineffective.

"I go back with Raymond as far as 1973," she said, "when I sought him out because I was concerned about hunger. We had lunch, and I asked him, 'What can one person do?' He said, 'Well you need to understand the food stamp program.' He spent lunchtime explaining food stamps, and how essential it was for poor people to get them. Then he said, very matter-of-factly, 'Now, what you need to do is to find everybody who needs food stamps in Mecklenburg County, sign them up, document the problems involved in the process, and then go to Washington and get the regulations changed.' He said it with such matter-of-factness," Mrs. Waller concluded, "that you just felt compelled to do it."

So she did it—leading a group of volunteers who, in a year's time, increased Mecklenburg's food stamp participation from 30 percent of those who were eligible to more than 95 percent.

Such dogged practicality, which Wheeler expected of himself as well as others, was a learned art for him—polished, in part, through his associations with Robert Kennedy.

After his hunger tours of Mississippi in 1967, Wheeler and his fellow physician, Harvard psychiatrist Robert Coles, arrived at Kennedy's office and passed on to the senator from New York depressing reports of their findings. Coles has told his Harvard classes of Kennedy's response—how he informed the doctors, politely, that their reports were essentially worthless unless they rolled up their sleeves, testifying on TV and laying themselves on the line before hostile Senate committees.

He suggested that Wheeler be the spokesman, since he had a Southern accent. Wheeler agreed, a trifle reluctantly perhaps, for his preference—like Coles—was to return to his practice. But he appeared before Congress and sparred with Southern senators, a knot in his stomach until he took a break for lunch.

"I had a martini," he later told a friend, "and when I testified again that afternoon, I never enjoyed myself so much in my life."

Wheeler had become annoyed during the lunchtime recess, angered by the charges of Mississippi's senators, James Eastland and John Stennis, that his morning testimony had been "gross libel and slander." So he returned to the witness table in the early afternoon, and speaking without notes, in a voice so calm and even that it was almost a monotone, but just a shade too intense for that description to really fit, this is what he said to the people in the room:

"I am distressed and concerned that Senators Eastland and Stennis interpret my remarks as libelous to the state of Mississippi. I was born and reared and educated in the South. I love the region as much as they do. I reported what I saw because it is intolerable to me that this situation should exist in the region I love. I saw those children and their parents, and I told you what I saw, and the message of helplessness and despair which they communicated to me.

"For the past 20 years, I have worked in the South, my birthplace and my home. During that time I have come to know in depth the white and the Negro—their problems, their sorrows, their joys. Throughout those years, my heart has wept for the South, as I have watched the Southern black man and white man walk their separate ways, distrusting each other, separated by false and ridiculous barriers—doomed to a way of life tragically less than they deserve, when, by working together, they could achieve a society finer and more successful than any which exists in this country today.

"And through all of that dreadful pageant of ignorance and suspicion and mutual distrust, the most distressing figure of all has been the Southern political leader who has exploited all of our human weaknesses for his own personal and selfish gain—refusing to grant us the dignity and the capability of responding to noble and courageous leadership—when all of us had nothing to lose but the misery and desolation which surround our lives.

"The time has come when this must cease. For we are concerned with little children, whose one chance for a healthy and productive existence—into which they were born—is at stake. I invite Sen. Eastland and Sen. Stennis to come with me to the vast farmlands of the delta and I will show you the children of whom we have spoken. I will show you their bright eyes and innocent faces, their shriveled arms and swollen bellies, their sickness and pain and the fear and misery of their parents. Their story must be believed, not only for their sakes but for the sake of all America."

When he had finished, the huge, polished hearing room was silent. Then the presiding senator, Joseph Clark of Pennsylvania, said: "Sen. Eastland, would you care to ask any questions?"

"I have no questions," Eastland said.

Clark turned to Stennis. "I have no questions," the senator said.

Wheeler rarely recounted such episodes to his friends—almost never talked of his speeches and pronouncements. Partly, he never considered himself very good with words. But more than that, it was a simple reluctance—an almost total inclination not to talk about himself.

"He was so modest," says William Porter, "that he never told you what he was doing. He'd disappear for three days and you'd find out where he had been in the *New York Times* or the *New Republic*. A lot of people do it for the cause," concluded Porter, "but they want to show their slides. Raymond didn't. He never let ego or convenience get in the way. He would not consider himself a Christian, I'm sure. But Raymond was really the ultimate selfless giver."

CHAPTER 11

Farewell to the Grand Dragon

The Ku Klux Klan is a cyclical organization. Sometimes it is violent and highly visible—as it was in the late 1970s and early '80s, a time culminating in the fatal Greensboro shootout between Klansmen and Communists. Only a few years earlier, however, the Klan was in disarray; membership was off, leaders were discouraged.

It was during that time that one of the Klan's most powerful members, Grand Dragon Bob Jones of North Carolina, decided to quit. I profiled him for the Race Relations Reporter magazine, asking him to reflect on his passion for white supremacy. The article was co-authored by Luisita Lopez, former national editor and now assistant managing editor of the Charlotte Observer. What comes through in it, I think, is the peculiar juxtaposition of Jones's humanity and his hideous racial views—a reminder, it seems, that the South's worst dilemmas were created, ironically, by basically decent people.

November, 1973

GRANITE QUARRY, N.C.—"You looking for old Bob Jones, the Grand Dragon?"

At the crossroads filling station, three men were sipping their early morning vending-machine coffee, a steady look in their eyes, wondering what a couple of city-dressed strangers wanted with their most famous neighbor. It was still some weeks before J. Robert Jones had shocked the semi-clandestine world of the Ku Klux Klan by resigning as Grand Dragon, giving in a little to his growing sense of fatigue, but also to a restless ambition he had nurtured for quite a while: a desire to try his hand at a more traditional form of politics and run for the state legislature.

It should come easy to him. Jones, by virtue of a decade as head of the potent North Carolina Klan, is already regarded with the same sort of protective awe that many of the state's back-country whites normally reserve for governors and U.S. senators. He is one of them, and yet he is not one of them, and everyday people such as the three men at the filling station are reluctant indeed to facilitate any outside intrusions upon his privacy.

Finally, however, after a respectable period of scrutiny, one member of the group sighed with a sort of what-the-hell resignation, slapped his denim-covered thigh, and reeled off directions.

Right off the bumpy unpaved road in the countryside of Granite Quarry, a one-main-street town of modest brick homes and 1,500 people, is Bob Jones's house, built with his own hands seven years ago. It resembles a long cinder-block mobile home, pale green, with a flat roof covered with the lightning rods he sells. A large weathered plywood sign with the words "Dragon's Den" hand-painted in green hangs out front.

Jones, as usual, had been up since dawn. He had been waiting at the kitchen table, already into his fourth cup of coffee. The ashtray was heaping with ashes and Belair butts. Jones had squeezed his ample, 240-pound frame between the wall and the table and was sitting under a KKK-decal-covered cuckoo clock whose hands had stopped moving some time ago. His hands trembled almost imperceptibly as he smoked a cigarette.

Jones is an intense man, full of stamina and hustle, although at 44, his brown hair is graying fast. He had become, in his latter days as Grand Dragon, a little less likely to jump into his big 1972 Chrysler and take himself a 200-mile drive, which he used to do routinely not so many years ago, when the Klan was thriving and a come-help phone call from a buddy across the state was all the encouragement he needed.

"I've driven a million miles," he explained with what he considers justifiable pride. "That's a hundred thousand miles every year I was Grand Dragon. I suppose I've made a coupla' thousand speeches, not only at rallies, but before church groups and on college campuses—talking mostly about drugs and communism. I was speaking at Pfeiffer College," he added, "the night Martin Luther King was killed."

The latter information was imparted with an air of gravity, as if it were an historical footnote to an enormously important event. Asked how he felt at the time, Jones became pensive, then stared across the kitchen table and said, "Well, I was just glad as hell it didn't happen in North Carolina, or they'd have damn sure tried to blame it on the Klan. King was just living on borrowed time anyway. He had stepped on too many toes."

On their face, the words—containing no evaluation either pro or con that a man whom Jones disliked intensely had been murdered—had a callous, almost indifferent ring. But his tone suggested there was more he wasn't saying, as if his apparent detachment was a cover for a profound ambivalence. It could be. One member of the Pfeiffer audience that night, who coincidentally is a neighbor of Jones's from five miles up the road, recalls that the Grand Dragon was well into his standard spiel when someone handed him a note about the assassination. Jones read it quietly, the neighbor said, and then

looked up and made a solemn announcement to the shaken crowd. "He seemed," she added, "as stunned and subdued as the rest of us."

But five years after the fact, Jones did not want to talk about it, and he shifted the subject, abruptly and a little eerily, to a bear hunting trip he and some buddies will soon take into the tangled, low-country woodlands of eastern North Carolina. These days, he explained, he takes considerable time out to hunt, as well as to grow an orchard by the side of the house, and to travel around the state selling his lightning rods. It is a profession, he added, that is not exactly making him rich, but helps him and his family live comfortably, enough for paneled walls, a 27-inch color TV and four cars.

And, of course, he keeps up with the Klan. Out in the back, he has two rooms cluttered with Klan literature, knick-knacks, and pro-Klan articles, mostly churned out by Klan members and published in obscure little papers. Jones steadfastly refuses to read the major state newspapers because, he says, the press never tells the truth. The truth being, for him, that the Klan is a moral and Christian organization, perhaps the last one left on earth.

James Robert Jones was born into the Klan. His father was a Southern Railroad worker who joined the 1920s Klan and his mother belonged to the Ladies Auxiliary. Jones was one of eight children, growing up in the Depression, in a family dogged by poverty and hard times—"Everybody had hard times those days," he says without a trace of self-pity. And he doesn't talk of the string of bad luck that struck the family: a sister killed by a stray bullet, a brother accidentally hit on the head by a baseball bat, his own car wreck that left him with a limp.

He attributes his fervor to the Klan not to the poverty of his early years, but to his parents. He grew up hearing his father and mother scorn blacks, pounding into him the notion that all too many of them were shiftless and mean, like "white trash."

"A lot of people get uncomfortable when they hear me talk about niggers," Jones said, pouring himself still another cup of coffee. "They don't like the word. Well, let me tell you something, there are niggers in the world, just like there are white trash. There are low down people of all kinds. Trouble is people who aren't from around here think when I say 'nigger' I mean all black people. Well, I don't. There are black people, or colored people, call them what you want, who are just as fine as anyone you could meet. I've had colored friends for years, and I'm damn proud of them."

"Fella up the road here called me one time right after he heard I had been elected Grand Dragon," Jones continued, warming to his subject. "Black fella. He said, 'Bob, have you got a minute?' I said, 'you know I do.' He said, 'well, how about coming up here to the house; I got something I want to talk to you about.' I said, 'Okay, you tell your wife to put some coffee on and I'll be right over.'

"I got there, and we sat in his kitchen drinking coffee, and he said, 'Bob, I heard you been elected Grand Dragon.' I said, 'Yessir, I have.' He looked me straight in the eyes, and he said, 'Bob, we been friends a long time.' I said, 'Yessir, we have.' He said, 'I hope this won't affect our friendship.' I said, 'Not as far as I'm concerned it won't, no sir.' We shook hands on it, and we've been friends ever since."

"Trouble is not the colored people," Jones concluded. "Trouble is the radicals and niggers."

The growing power of radicals throughout the 1960s and into this decade buttressed Jones's decision, reached when he was still a young man, to devote his life to the Klan. And even in his waning days as Grand Dragon, he would spend hours plotting ways to breathe the life back into the organization.

Immediately before he stepped down, he insisted he was leaving the KKK in good shape. "We're still growing," he said. "Sure the crowds are smaller. People get more complacent when the going gets rough,' meaning that the clear-cut, explosive issues of the 1960s are now diffused. You can't grab at them. There are no marches on Selma, no restaurant sit-ins, no freedom riders in Mississippi. But for Bob Jones the eternal issue is the rights of white people—which, he contended, are still in serious jeopardy.

"The Klan is the only organization working for the rights of white American Protestants," he said. "The Catholics have the Knights of Columbus, the Jews have B'nai B'rith, the niggers got the NAACP. But who have we got?"

He knew the spiel by rote. He had repeated it at almost every rally, every press conference, every interview over the past decade. It came off in private conversation with the force of a tape-recording. He seemed to know it and quickly changed the subject.

He proceeded to dig out old photos stored alongside the dusty antique glass he has piled up in the cramped and cluttered room out back he uses for an office. "Here I am with the Imperial Wizard," he boasted of his photo with Alabama's Robert Shelton. And though there have long been rumors of jealousy between the two (they are the Klan's two best known figures), there was no trace of bad feeling in Jones's voice.

He strolled from his office back to the house, through the den, where three shotguns and a half a dozen portraits of himself in his Grand Dragon robe were hanging. Beaming with pride, he brought out of his huge bedroom closet the $40 emerald-green satin robe. "I've worn out several of these," he said, smiling with a countryman's brusque amiability.

There is no doubt Bob Jones is proud of his role in the building of the North Carolina Klan. For it, he traveled exhaustingly across the state, organizing units, collecting dues and recruiting. He skipped meals, got a troublesome stomach and ran on what he calls "nervous energy." He says he slept only twice a week. Finally, he went to prison for the Klan.

In 1969, he was tried and convicted for contempt of Congress and sentenced by U.S. District Judge John J. Sirica to federal prison in Danbury, Conn. Jones's refusal to turn over Klan records to the House Un-American Activities Committee cost him 10 months behind bars.

He can be bitter about the months in jail, and bitter also about the other forms of governmental reprisal and coercion he says have been heaped upon the Klan, not only in North Carolina, but throughout the South. He maintained, for example, that just before his trial, a representative from the U.S. Department of Justice arrived at his house to offer him a deal. "I wish to hell I had gotten that fella's name," he said, recalling his disgust. "He told me that if I would resign from the Klan and denounce it, they would give me a suspended sentence. I told the bureaucratic son-of-a-bitch to get himself and his briefcase off my property."

Jones points out that the Justice Department at about the same time offered a similar deal to Georgia's Grand Dragon, Calvin Craig, who took it, denounced the Klan, joined a Model Cities governing board, and became an instant folk hero to some liberal journalists. "That's okay," said Jones, "it ain't me who has to look at Calvin Craig's face in the mirror every morning."

"Course," he added, "the government, particularly the FBI, has done a lot worse." He proceeded to recount the broad outlines of a 1968 incident in Mississippi, which had been painstakingly documented two years after it happened by *Los Angeles Times* correspondent, Jack Nelson. According to Nelson's story, which was carried in full by only two newspapers in the country (the *Times* and the *Washington Post*), Jewish leaders from the Anti-Defamation League in Meridian, Miss., conspired with the FBI to create a trap aimed at killing two Mississippi Klan leaders, Thomas Tarrants and Danny Joe Hawkins.

Nelson reported that the ADL had raised $38,500 which was paid to two Klan informers and a middleman in return for their help in setting the trap. The two informers, Raymond and Wayne Alton Roberts, were to persuade Tarrants and Hawkins to place a bomb at the home of a Jewish businessman, Meyer Davidson. Law enforcement officials, according to Nelson, were to be waiting, and many of them did not expect either Tarrants or Hawkins to emerge from the incident alive.

There had been, prior to the setting of the trap, a rash of bombings affecting the homes and businesses of Meridian blacks and Jews, and all available evidence pointed squarely to the Klan. The trap was seen as the most effective solution to an already deadly problem.

When Tarrants arrived at the Davidson home at 1:00 a.m., June 30, 1968, law enforcement officers—10 FBI agents and 12 Meridian policemen—were stunned to see that Hawkins was not with him. In his place, was a young Klanswoman named Kathy Ainsworth. In reconstructing the episode, Nelson reported that Tarrants got out of the car with a bomb made of dynamite in his hands and a pistol stuck in his belt. Exactly what happened next is a matter of dispute, but in any case, shooting broke out right away, and Mrs. Ainsworth was killed. Tarrants were seriously wounded, but recovered and was sentenced to 30 years in Mississippi's Parchman Prison. He was 21 at the time.

"Here in North Carolina, it's been a little different," Jones said. "The government's most common weapon was economic reprisal. A awful lot of my boys would lose their jobs because the government had leaned on their employers."

"In the summer of 1965," Jones recalled with a mixture of anger and satisfaction, "Pepsi Cola Company fired four drivers because of their Klan affiliation. So on July 4, we distributed flyers all over the place, telling people a little something about Pepsi Cola."

What the flyers asserted was that one of the company's national vice-presidents was a black man who had married a white woman. "We titled it, 'the saddest story ever told,'" Jones remembered with obvious relish. "It damn near ruined their sales for a good long while, and they finally came to me, and said, 'Bob, what can we do to get you off our backs?' I told 'em," Jones added, laughing, "'You can pay my damn printing costs.'"

He seems mellower about all that now, regarding the hassles and his own year in prison as something of a badge of distinction, an ordeal by fire. "I'm writing a book about that year," he said, and to prove he wasn't kidding, he showed off the cover of his book, a framed pencil sketch done by a fellow convict. The crudely done sketch depicted a drowning man and the tearful face of a woman watching. "It means the tears of your family," Jones said. "The drowning man is me."

Jones is a sentimental man, a tough but affectionate father. "My wife and me been married 22 years and it's been good," he said. "Now my daughter Sheila is getting married, and I've built her a house across the road. We like to stay close together."

Jones likes to needle Sheila, a friendly, attractive 19-year-old, warning her gruffly that there would be no wedding unless boyfriend Danny trimmed his long blond hair. Sheila, thin and talkative, plainly adored her dad, teasing back and going her own way cheerfully.

While the banter in the kitchen went on, Jones's wife quietly dried the dishes and emptied ashtrays. "Syble here," he motions toward his trim, dignified wife—whom he commonly refers to as "the boss"—"Syble is the third best lady segregationist speaker in the nation. And Sheila finished high school and is working at a factory making $2.95 an hour."

"She doesn't need to go to college making that kind of money," he bragged.

Money, politics, power. Bob Jones, like many self-made men, frankly clamors for these. He has decided, he said, to run for the North Carolina General Assembly this spring, confident that he stands a good chance of winning. "I've got a built-in base," he explained. "People know who I am."

He began to speak of the politicians the Klan has endorsed and probably helped elect: sheriffs, small-town councilmen and mayors, and U.S. Sen. Jesse Helms. "The Klan can throw weight around any time it wants to," he said. But he did not mention that in 1963, admittedly before his rise to celebrity status, he ran for the Board of Aldermen in Granite Quarry, his hometown. He came in last with 66 votes.

Still talking politics, he walked outside to the carport, the screen door to the kitchen flapping behind him. He stopped to pat his month-old Pekingese puppy, unabashedly affectionate, cooing about "my newest baby," then looked with pride over the surrounding fields he owns. And he pointed to the license tag on his car—UKA-1. "It pays to advertise," he laughed.

Eight years ago, Jones would have scoffed at advertising. He didn't need it. Those were the glory days of the modern Klan, the mid-1960s, when rallies in cow pastures and corn fields would draw thousands of believers and Jones was treated like the godfather of white supremacy. North Carolina was described as "Klansville, U.S.A.," and Jones was seriously regarded by some worried government officials as the rising star of the United Klans of America, perhaps the next Imperial Wizard.

Jones was able to drum up blood-curdling fervor from the traditional supporters of the Klan: farmers, laborers, working-class people, a smattering of sheriff's deputies, small-town businessmen and work-toughened mill hands.

At its peak in the 1960s, the North Carolina Klan with its Ladies Auxiliary counted at least 6,000 dues-paying members and claimed thousands of sympathizers. Now, even the most optimistic estimate of Klan membership is only 500, and much lower estimates are common. But given the cyclical nature of the 117-year-old organization and its ability to flourish in an atmosphere of social discord, Jones had ample reason to hope that the emotions that nourish the Klan were, even in the complex 1970s, once again ready for the plucking.

Those hopes brought him in late summer to a UKA rally down east at Castle Hayne, a roadside town of trailer parks, gas stations and a few rambling general stores near Wilmington in New Hanover County, long a Klan stronghold. It was a muggy, overcast Saturday afternoon, and Jones, in a shiny brown-striped business suit and fashionably wide tie, was the main attraction, busy pumping hands, greeting newcomers with the affable flair and charm of an accomplished Southern politician.

"You know," somebody told him, tugging at his big arm, "you could have been a great politician, you know that."

"Yeah," Jones replied with a boyish smile, "I'm lovable."

But after seven unsuccessful attempts on his life, he realizes that not everyone finds him so, and he was, as usual, carrying a Smith & Wesson .38 pistol in a shoulder holster beneath his tightly buttoned coat. He insists, however, that he doesn't like violence or the talk of it, and even his detractors will admit that Jones himself did not encourage some of the terror tactics—including murder—that the Klan was blamed for. "You may think this is a story," Jones says with a level gaze, "but I have never participated in any violence while I was Grand Dragon or told anybody else to do it." But Jones frankly acknowledges that, being a man of some bluster, he has sometimes threatened to employ as much force as necessary, and on many of those occasions, he says, he wasn't bluffing.

"I remember back in 1966, my number two man died, and we had the biggest Klan funeral ever in North Carolina. We buried him up at National Cemetery in Salisbury, and the Defense Department wasn't too happy about it. Well, I said 'listen here you sumbitches, this man was in the Air Force for 24 years, and he's damn sure entitled to be buried in a military cemetery.' So then they tried to turn it into a military funeral instead of a Klan funeral. They tried to say he couldn't be buried in his Klan robe, and they sent a firing squad for a military, 21-gun salute."

As Jones continued with the story, some of the anger of the day seemed to come back to him, and the narrative became more and more intense. "I told them," he said, his voice taking on a clipped, stacatto coldness, "that we had our own Klan firing squad for the salute, and I said, 'besides, you got a ape in your firing squad, and if he sets foot in this cemetery, I'm gonna kill that nigger.' Fortunately, they backed off."

Asked if he really would have killed the black soldier, Jones replied with no hesitation at all, "Does a duck waddle?"

"Sometimes," he went on, sounding a little more philosophical now, "force, or the threat of it, is the only language people understand. We had a situation here in Granite Quarry only a short time back where there was fighting between black kids and white kids. We never had that before in this town, we always believed in getting along here, but the way I heard it, the black kids were beating up on the white kids for no reason at all.

"So I went to this black friend of mine, fella I had known a long time, and I said, 'Listen here, me and you got to do something about this.' I said, 'I'm gonna do some checking, and if I find out it's the white kids' fault, I'm gonna whip their ass. And if you find out it's the black kids' fault, you make 'em stop, because if they don't, I'm gonna get me a baseball bat and break some elbows and knees, and can't none of them play football with broken elbows and knees.' Well, we haven't had a bit of trouble since."

Jones admits the method may seem a bit crude, but he said it accomplished something he insists has long been one of his priorities as Grand Dragon: keeping things as cool as possible. Not all Klansmen share that goal, and that fact underlay one recent episode that figured in Jones's decision to resign.

"The unit up at Edenton wanted to have a rally not long ago," he said, "but there had been some racial tension up there, so I wouldn't approve it. I couldn't see us going and making things worse. Well, the boys up there went to Bobby Shelton (the Imperial Wizard and national head of the Klan), and he approved it. When your own people start going over your head," Jones added, "it's time to step aside."

But at the Castle Hayne rally late in the summer, he showed no signs of planning to quit; he just seemed a little uptight over the size of the crowd.

He was smoking heavily, glancing at his watch nervously, and blaming the gray clouds and the soggy trailerpark field for the thin turnout. The clouds hovered over the field all afternoon and into the evening. Jones, the only man in a suit, had tiny drops of sweat at the temples.

"Wait 'til the sky gets black," he mused to no one in particular. "Some of the boys are scared to be seen out here in the daylight. They've got jobs to worry about."

But the sky darkened and a light shower fell and only a dozen more cars drove in and parked alongside the heavy late models clustered by the leaking tent where burgers were sizzling on charcoal grills. At the other end of the tent, where most of the crowd of about 75 people mingled, an old man reeking of liquor approached Bob Jones. "Bob, I wanna be a member. I wanna thank you for what you done." Jones shook the man's hand and directed him to somebody else. Then turning to a companion, Jones whispered: "That old man is a drunk. We don't need people like that."

Trying to hide his contempt for the drinkers in the crowd, Jones mixed, patting children on the head, holding babies in his arms, walking around quickly, his limp barely noticeable. His pale brown eyes, bloodshot with fatigue from lack of sleep and the six-hour drive from his home, darted over the crowd. He walked to the flatbed truck to address the group. A frown deepened the lines on his tanned face.

"Look at you," he commanded the crowd, his voice rising, "the country's going to hell, your children are driven to nigger schools, the government's telling you to live with niggers and make love to them, and what are you people doing about it? Where are the people of New Hanover County, the people who care?"

When he had finished he heaved down from the truck and paused at a group of friends. "Hell, that crowd's terrible," he mumbled, and then signaled off hand for the burning of the cross.

The cross, grounded into the middle of the field, was 35 feet high, a telephone pole and cross beam wrapped in burlap. Security guards and a few Ladies Auxiliary members touched it with their burning torches as the crowd gathered quietly to watch. For a brief time, eerie flames reflected off the passive faces, but soon it was over and no one stayed to watch the smoldering cross burn out.

Looking back on all that now, Jones seems, despite his pride and nostalgia, relieved to be out of it. "Nah, I won't miss it," he says. "After a million miles and a thousand speeches, I think I deserve to step down."

But he also admits that his restless energy needs a channel, and he says he hopes to find it in politics. "I want to run for the legislature for one reason and one reason only," he explains. "We have a terrible drug problem in this state, and I want to see us enact tough laws to combat it."

"That," he added with a level, peculiar gaze, "is something that could benefit both black and white alike."

Bob Jones has never been elected to office. Neither has he resumed his leadership role in the Klan. The KKK of the '80s is a violent organization. That is not his inclination.

CHAPTER 12

The Dreams of Gilbert Blue

Gilbert Blue, chief of South Carolina's Catawba Indians, is a man caught up in an improbable notion—that he and his people can regain some of the land that was taken from them, and then use it as a base to re-establish their identity. That identity is a subtle thing, involving a feeling for the land, a profound sense of place and a patient, long-run understanding of history that is foreign to most of us in 20th-century America. All of that has sustained Gilbert Blue through a protracted dispute, bitter at times, that shows no signs of ending.

January, 1982

There's a part of Gilbert Blue that dreads these times, when the phone starts ringing and the reporters come around and his evenings with his family become even more scarce.

Blue is a large, gentle man—an easy-going machinist with a 10th-grade education—and he hates controversy. It tears at him, sends him wandering through the woods where he prays and meditates and tries to keep his head straight.

But he asked for it, of course. You don't assert ancient claims to 144,000 acres of prime real estate—chunks of towns and subdivisions and rolling timber country—without attracting attention. So on a recent afternoon, gray and drizzly in South Carolina, he tried without enthusiasm, but with unfailing politeness, to explain the issues as he understands them.

Blue, 48, is chief of what's left of the Catawba Indian tribe. He looks the part with his dark wavy hair and deeply tan skin, and he has thought a lot about what it means to be an Indian.

"It's an inner thing," he explains in a baritone voice that is friendly and easy-going. "I meditate a lot and go out in the woods to think. I think about being a part of nature, and that my people were here before anyone else."

That sense of attachment, not only to the land, but to a particular piece of it, has become more and more important to Gilbert Blue. It has left him today with an improbable aspiration: He'd like to restore the Catawba Nation—to see the 1200 people now on the tribal rolls reestablish the prosperity and cohesion of a few centuries back.

It will not be easy. Today, the Catawba reservation is one square mile—about 640 acres of pitted clay roads and barren-looking forests, a few mobile homes and some cramped frame houses just south of Rock Hill. But if Blue has his way—and eventually he may—some of that will change. Buoyed by the success of the Penobscot Indians in the wilderness of northern Maine, he and the Catawbas have reasserted claim to their shrunken homeland.

In 1976, they announced that under a treaty signed with England in 1760, they were the rightful owners of 144,000 acres in South Carolina—an area including much of York County and spilling into neighboring Chester and Lancaster Counties.

They asked for a settlement involving land and money. In the five years since, after futile negotiations about how much they should get, the issue has made its way into U.S. District Court.

The Catawbas sued 87 defendants, including city and county governments, industries and individuals. A ruling is expected soon, but it won't decide much. It will center on an issue that is essentially procedural, and the losing side is almost certain to appeal.

Still, it has served to rekindle some interest, and recently Blue found himself conducting a tour of the reservation, philosophizing a little about the struggles of his people. He began with some history—how they drifted down from the Ohio Valley more than 500 years ago, while their ancient cousins, the Sioux, moved west to the Dakotas. Until the 18th century, the Catawbas were proud and mighty, roaming through the woodlands of what became the Carolinas.

But after Europeans arrived in their vast hunting lands, the Catawbas, like other tribes, fared poorly. They fought for the British during the French and Indian War, and their ranks were thinned by battlefield losses. Then Scotch-Irish settlers moved into their territory, bringing a smallpox virus that killed still more of the tribe.

In 1760, trying to preserve what he could, the Catawba Chief Arataswa signed the Treaty of Pine Hill. He gave up all the tribal hunting lands except for 15 square miles in what is now York County.

Blue contends that treaty still applies—that it was sealed into U.S. law in 1790. He acknowledges that in 1840, the Catawbas gave up their remaining lands in a treaty with South Carolina. But he contends the 1840 treaty was illegal because Congress never approved it, which federal law required, and South Carolina never fully honored it.

Until about 10 years ago, such legal reasoning might have seemed tenuous at best, the precedents too ancient to have much application. But then the Penobscot Indians—backed by a Colorado-based public interest law firm called the Native American Rights Fund (NARF), and later by the U.S. Department of Interior—successfully asserted their

claim to two-thirds of Maine. They accepted a $37 million settlement.

At a meeting of eastern Indians in the early 1970s, Blue met Don Miller, an aggressive young lawyer for the NARF, and Miller pointed out the legal similarities between the Catawbas and Penobscots.

Blue was elated, and not simply at the possibility of winning land and money. He also saw the chance of restoring tribal identity, which had faded badly by the late 20th century. Nobody spoke the Catawba language anymore, nobody seemed to care about the ancient tribal dances, and after years of intermarriage, there were no Catawba full-bloods.

Until the 1960s, Blue himself gave little thought to such matters. But then he returned home after nine years in the Navy. He had sampled the cultures of China, Australia, South America and the Philippines, and he was becoming interested in his own.

He began to think about his grandfather, Samuel Taylor Blue, a slender man, about 6 foot 1, with high Indian cheekbones and jet-black hair. Beginning in the early 20th century, the elder Blue was chief of the Catawbas for about 40 years.

Samuel Taylor Blue was a steadfast believer in Indian identity. He still spoke the language, and occasionally he would take his grandson on walks through the woods, talking to him earnestly about the traditions of his people, trying to pass along what it means to be Catawba.

"I wish I had listened to him a little closer," Blue said as he strolled through an old reservation cemetery recently, crunching through the briars and the carpet of oak leaves, peering at inscriptions on the fading gravestones.

Blue resembles his grandfather. He is tall and imposing, with steady dark eyes, and he wears outward symbols of the heritage he values—a beadwork necklace, an Indian-head tattoo on his left forearm.

The growing sense of identity is at the heart of Blue's motives in the current land claim. He wants to expand the reservation, then use it as the focal point for a tribal self-respect—a place where Indians can live and hunt, grow crops, build industries and reestablish a satisfaction in who they are and were.

"Our people would never have been in poverty," says Blue, "if we had had our land."

There are those who regard Blue's dreams as quixotic, even potentially destructive—out of touch, in the end, with 20th-century realities. One is Guy Johnston, who lives on five acres in York County.

Johnston is a computer operations manager, a man with a thoughtful demeanor who helped organize a group called the Tri-County Landowners Association, which for the past several years has resisted the Catawba claim.

He accepts absolutely Gilbert Blue's sincerity, respects his persistence and his gentlemanly personality. But on behalf of his fellow non-Indians, Johnston also contends with considerable force and logic: "We have committed no crime, and we are not in the wrong."

He sees no reason, therefore, that he and others like him should lose their land.

"No person alive today should be held accountable for possible wrongs by our ancestors," says Johnston. "If we were, we'd all be in jail for slavery."

Blue is sympathetic to Johnston's feelings. He insists he doesn't want to force land owners off the land, and he has tried to do what he can to be reassuring.

"No matter what kind of settlement we end up with," he has said many times, "we are not going to take developed land, shopping centers. That's not our intention. We're not going to get condemnation rights. People who own the land now bought it in good faith. We're not trying to push anybody out, and we're not being radical. But the land is rightfully ours, and we are going to negotiate for the best settlement we can get."

Despite Blue's gentle rhetoric, the Catawba claim has cast a pall over real estate development in much of York County. Some land titles have "Catawba exceptions"—stipulations, in effect, that the titles may not apply if the Indians win their case. And as Johnson notes, even if Blue rejects the idea of condemnation—the legal seizure of land against the owner's wishes—it is still conceivable that some court could order it.

For all those reasons, Blue was prepared for the idea that non-Indians would resist him. What stunned him for a while was that many Catawbas did, too. They agreed, to be sure, that the tribe had been wronged. But lacking Blue's obsession with Catawba identity and history, they wanted money, not land, as a settlement for the claim.

There was logic in their choice. Many of them were poor—a group of struggling rural people who needed the money, and who had little patience with the dreams of Gilbert Blue.

At first, Blue simply defended his position. "I, for one," he said in 1978, "am not going to sell my heritage for any amount. We deserve something as a people, not as individuals. I think the Catawba Nation has been wronged. Not Gilbert Blue individually."

During 1977-78, however, the anti-Blue forces were clearly gaining momentum. The factionalism complicated, and eventually helped to kill, out-of-court negotiations between the Indians and the government.

Gilbert Blue became equally discouraged. For the first time since his election as chief in 1973, he thought seriously of stepping down. But in the end, he simply compromised. He agreed to seek cash payments for individuals, along with an expanded land base for the Catawba reservation, federal money for a tribal development fund and federal recognition of the Catawbas' tribal status.

The pro-cash Catawbas accepted the compromise, prompting Blue to proclaim in early 1980: "We're closer together now than we've ever been as a tribe."

So what does the future hold? What are the chances the Catawba claim will succeed, and how long will it take for the issue to be decided?

Blue would like to see it happen soon. He says he spends too little time with his supportive wife, Libby, and three teenage children. And he has other interests as well. He is an ordained Mormon minister and plays country music with a York County band. But he knows the legal struggle could last a lot longer—maybe eight or 10 more years, he thinks—before the appeals and court decisions play themselves out.

By most people's standards, that seems a long time. But on a certain level, it doesn't to Blue. He seems, somehow, to have retained an Indian's sense of time, a belief in the cyclical nature of history. For more than a hundred years, his people have been caught on the cycle's down side, their homeland vanishing, their identity fading steadily. But it's all an eyeblink in the great sweep of history, and Blue says he's certain their day will come again.

"This is not something we undertook just recently," he says of the land claim. "Immediately after the 1840 treaty, we knew we had been cheated. It's just that not until a few years ago did our people have the education and leadership to pursue this.

"I don't have any great concerns about not winning our case. It's just a matter of time. It's just a matter of waiting."

CHAPTER 13

The Death Row Preacher

In 1980, when I was working on a story about Will Campbell (chapter three), I paid a visit to Death Row in Tennessee. Campbell is a staunch opponent of capital punishment, seeing it as simply another piece in the escalation of violence in America.

While the morality of the death penalty may be genuinely complicated, this much is clear: Strapping people to electric chairs and pumping enough electricity through their bodies to set their flesh on fire is a violent thing to do—as coolly calculated and utterly premeditated as killing ever is.

After talking to a half dozen Death Row inmates in Tennessee and several more in other states, I developed a kind of macabre fascination for the doomed men and women of our society. Many of them are terrifying people. That's why they are facing death. But others seem remarkably ordinary, and one of the people in the latter category is Bill Groseclose in Tennessee.

I met Grosecose in 1980 and have visited him four times since then. I found him articulate, funny, sensitive and mostly cheerful —all of which surprised me. I don't mean to idealize him. He may be guilty of one of the most hideous murders in the recent history of Tennessee. On the other hand, he may be innocent.

His trial was sloppy and he was poorly represented. But that is not my point in the story that follows. I am simply convinced that Groseclose is worth knowing—particularly to those of us who plan to kill him by proxy.

Whatever else you can say about him—and in this piece I let him speak for himself—Groseclose puts a human face on an unsavory abstraction, one that most of us try not to think about.

June, 1982

Unless something changes, they're going to kill Bill Groseclose before very much longer. It'll go something like this: Some people he barely knows will lead him from his cell at the Tennessee State Prison. They'll strap him to a tall, wooden chair and attach some electrodes to his thighs and so forth. Already, they'll have shaved his head to keep his hair from catching fire. Then they'll pull a switch, which will send maybe 2500 volts of electricity through his body.

Nobody knows how bad it will hurt, since nobody has ever reported back after the experience. But if recent precedents hold true, several things are likely. Groseclose's flesh, particularly around his legs, will begin to burn. His fists will clench involuntarily, and his hands will probably blacken. In addition, he might not die right away. If he doesn't they'll repeat the dosage as many times as it takes.

The people who do this will have very good reasons. They will know some of the details of Groseclose's history. They will know that he was arrested in 1977 after his wife was discovered in the trunk of a car. They will know that she was stabbed and raped and beaten, and they may also know that she did not die from those things. She cooked—probably over a period of several days— beneath the July sun in the river town of Memphis.

They will know these things, and they will feel that they are doing what they should—for theirs will be an awesome duty. But there are also things that they will not consider. Harmon Wray will consider them, and Abel Adams, but they will not be able to convince the people in authority. They will believe Bill Groseclose is innocent—that he is not vicious and cruel, and that he could never have done the things that the State says he did.

But they will not dwell on that point, for they are Christian ministers, and their interest is in redemption. So they will talk instead about Groseclose's life: his correspondence studies at a small Bible college, his ordination as a Church of God minister only a short time after his conviction for murder. They will try to tell the governor, who will not want to listen, about their conversations with Groseclose over five years.

They will use words like kindness, faith and humor, and they will speak of his desperate consolations in the writing of St. Paul. But they will certainly fail, for their words will have the soft and simple ring of sentimentality—and others in their grief will cry out for revenge, and time will pass slowly until his waiting will end.

II

Groseclose enters the room with a bounce to his step, clad in jeans, a T-shirt and a faded denim jacket; the numbers 83408 are stitched on the back. He is 34 years old, though he looks much younger. He wears wire-rimmed glasses and his hair and beard are scraggly. But the thing you notice most, and the thing that stays with you, is the lopsided grin.

Ask him a question or two, and his thoughts flow freely, the feelings tumbling out with punctuations of laughter, moving inexorably from the light to the heavy. This is what he says:

Man, it's cold in here—just about back up to the shivering point. We got a leak back there, and water comes pouring into the cell behind

the commode. Then it freezes on the wall in this little thin layer of ice that you can't really see.

So you're standing there in front of the john, and you've already started, and you lean against the wall, and zap, you're sliding all over the place, and the stream's goin' crazy, and you're laughing like a madman, and then you say to yourself, "Man, how weird can things get?"

It's hard sometimes, but everybody tries to keep each other up. It's just something everybody seems to do. If someone is down and he likes something on TV, someone will say something about that show. If that don't work, you're quiet for a half hour, then you try another subject. If that fails, you straight out ask, "Hey, man, what's happenin'?"

Always, always, you look for the humor. The hatred is there, it's a constant; you don't have to look for the hatred. But you do look for the way to laugh, and often enough we find it. We have a good sense of community.

Down the row there's Richard Austin; he plays cards—plays cards and gambles. He'll take bets on anything—football, baseball, basketball, how many bullets they'll shoot on Bonanza. He took fifth in the world billiard championships one time, but he hardly ever discusses playing pool. He keeps pretty much to himself. Got a bad heart.

Ole Richard, he's short and fat; he's balding and got this mustache. But he don't like to think of himself as fat. He'll say, "I am muscular. . . ." He's O.K.

I don't have one best friend. Everybody is pretty close. It's who are you hanging out with this week? I sat back there all day a while back and played chess with Houston—that's Richard Houston in the cell next to mine. It was one good, full, hard day of chess. It'll be a while before I do that again.

Houston is black. He's well-educated, very smart, a pretty handsome dude. We been next door neighbors for three years. One time—I forget what we was mad about—I cut out this cross out of an envelope, you know, then I licked it and stuck it to his door and set it on fire. So he cut himself out a cross, and for the next little while, he worked at it with a burned match, rubbing the carbon on the cross until the whole thing was black. Then he stuck it on my door.

Well, I couldn't let it drop at that point. So the next day, I painted a watermelon and stuck it on his door and burned it. Some of what we find to laugh about is pretty weird. But any time you can give somebody an excuse to laugh, you do it.

We don't start stirring till about 10 or 11—usually about the noon meal. Everybody just says no to breakfast. The dinner today was . . . well, how can I say it? Only one guy took anything. I've fed a lot of dogs a lot of things. But none of them were that bad.

The problem is time. Sometimes you don't know if you want it to pass, or you don't want it to pass. But it hangs pretty heavy sometimes. You'll do anything to fill it up. Jeff Dix down there, he placed third in the cockroach race. Jeff's a soap opera freak. We call him Swamp Monster. He's about 6-feet-2 and weighs 260 pounds. And a nose—man, Jimmy Durante would have to hide. This guy has a beak.

Jeff is a non-violent, violent person. He has weird ways of expressing himself. 'Course he says the same thing about me, but one time he put a TV set through the bars of his cell with one blow— plastic and tubes and crap all over the place. I just kept on with what I was doin', trying to be nonchalant, don't you know.

I paint a good bit, particularly with James Earl Ray. Ray's all right. He's a good guy. He's not on the row, but he's one of our best buddies. Me and him and Joe Buck paint together. Joe's the best portrait painter I ever seen. I can paint mountains in my sleep, 'cause that's where I was raised.

So we started painting this collective picture. Ray painted the sky and some clouds—he was experimenting with how to accent the clouds, whether to use reds or greens or whatever. Then he gave it to me to do the mountains, and I'll give it to Joe to do the foreground.

We got a good laugh out of trying to figure out a name to sign to the painting. We were trying to decide between Billy Joe Ray and Billy Buck Ray. We tried to imagine the painting hanging in some art gallery, and everybody sees it and can't wait to meet this Billy Buck Ray.

We don't want any trouble back here on the row. We've got all we can use. So we do what we can to help each other out, to keep each other's spirits boosted. We've got one back there who can't read and write. We're teachin' him. Whenever he gets a letter, we go over it with him. He reads the letter, then somebody else will read it, and they'll say, "O.K., what did it say?" He spits it back out. If he can't, we go over it with him.

Mostly, though, we just sit and watch the world go by. I've been behind bars five years. I was arrested July 11, 1977. I made it here in April, 1978—April Fool's Day. At first, it ate at me—especially with the situation as crazy as it is. But then you say, "What am I going to do about it? Am I going to scream or cry the rest of my life? What is going to come of it?"

So you have to learn to live with it. You have to get rid of the superflous, and you have to keep control of your mind. I have lost control a time or two. Of my mind, yes, and of my emotions. But I've been fortunate not to lose control of both at the same time.

Still, you think about things. Like sometimes I think about Vietnam. I was there in the Navy, and the things that happened, man . . . I mean the thing you ask yourself about Vietnam is, Why? You answer that a million times, and then you turn around and disregard the answer and say, Why?

One time when I was over there, I came upon this torture scene. I was driving a supply truck, and I came to a hut where this Vietnamese peasant had been castrated and tied to a tree. They stuck his penis in his mouth and sutured it shut. They had cut his wife's abdomen open and pulled out a fetus and used it to beat her children to death.

I stopped and said, "My God, human beings could not have done this to other human beings." Then I saw five Vietnamese regulars running up a hill behind the hut; they were giggling. I pulled my pistol and emptied it in their direction. I saw three go down. I said, "Did I, or didn't I?" Over the years, I had time to think. I asked myself, "Do I have so little control over my emotions I would shoot at somebody in a moment like that?"

I got more serious about religion in Vietnam. Death is so imminent, you can't really help it.

We also talk about it a lot on the row. About everybody back there is anti-religious. I don't mean by that that there aren't any believers. In fact, I don't think there are any non-believers. There's some that say, "No, I don't." But when the believers are having their conversations, there's always close attentiveness among the non-believers. They are the ones that keep the conversation alive. Opinions back there are straight from the heart and cold as ice.

The guys would see these ministers on TV with all their fallacies. Jerry Falwell is our pet. Oh, we love him. They're building some crap, and he's wanting me to send him $50 for one memorial brick, and for $500 he'll put gold on it or something. Or look at Oral Roberts with his multi-million dollar prayer tower. How many hungry kids could you feed for that?

But to err is human.

I've tried to put across the idea of Christianity vs. religion, and I think the general feeling back there is that religion is of man; it stinks. Christianity is of God; it's all right.

A lot of the guys have said, "if I was on the streets, more likely than not, I'd be just like 'em." But in here, it's a peculiar situation. In my case, it has strengthened my faith. I have not been confronted and bothered with the pressures of the outside world— with prices going up, or how am I going to make more money? I can devote more time to being still and listening.

I read the Bible a lot—underline verses and think about their meaning. Romans 8:18 is my favorite, but you can keep going from there. Ol' Paul could write: "I consider that what we suffer at this present time cannot be compared at all with the glory that is going to be revealed to us. For we know that up to the present time all of creation groans with pain, like the pain of childbirth.

"But it is not just creation alone which groans; we who have the Spirit as the first of God's gifts also groan within us for God to make us his sons and set our whole being free.

"If God is for us, who can be against us? . . . Who will accuse God's chosen people? God himself delcares them not guilty. Who, then, will condemn them? Who, then, can separate us from the love of Christ? Can trouble do it, or hardship or persecution or hunger or poverty or danger or death? . . .

"No in these things we have complete victory through he who loved us. For I am certain that nothing can ever separate us from his love; neither death nor life, neither angels nor other heavenly rulers or powers, neither the present or the future, neither the world above nor the world below—there is nothing in all creation that will ever be able to separate us from the love of God which is ours through Christ Jesus our Lord."

That's some pretty heavy stuff, and I think about it sometimes, and then I just listen. There's a difference, I've discovered, between wants and needs. I think I know that now. If I get out someday, there's a lot I'm looking forward to. But in or out, it's God's will that matters.

III

He was born in 1948 near Salt Lick, Va., growing up in a two-story house with twin chimneys and a covered porch on two sides. There was a good-climbing sugar maple near the picket fence out front, and he would climb to the point where the branches became frail and stare off at the colors on the mountain behind his house.

Boyhood had its idyllic moments, but there were also hard times. After his parents divorced, his mother, a round-faced woman with a receding chin like her son's, took a job as a payroll clerk at a gypsum mine. She lost it when the mine caved in, and after that, she moved around in search of other work. When Groseclose was 12, she remarried, and the family wound up in Kingsport, Tenn.

Her new husband, Walter Taylor, was short and heavyset—a storeroom worker at an Eastman Kodak plant, who learned from his stepson how to write his name. Groseclose says he and Taylor got along well—"I learned from him, he learned from me"—and adolescence passed with only normal scrapes and mischief.

At 17, Groseclose joined the Navy and spent four years in Vietnam. He survived and came home, and after a failed marriage that produced two children—freckle-faced boys now 10 and 8—he moved on to Memphis. He worked as a Navy recruiter, and on April 4, 1975, two years after his separation and divorce, he remarried.

His new wife, Deborah, was 5-feet-2, blond and rather pretty. "Like any marriage," says Groseclose, "this one had its problems. We had no joys or difficulties that other married couples don't experience."

They did fight, however, and on the night of June 28, 1977, they had quite a row. The next morning, Groseclose took his infant son for a routine trip to the doctor and then to the Navy office so they could pick up a paycheck. When he returned, his wife was gone. So was their green Plymouth Fury, a 1973 model. Groseclose says he wasn't worried, since Deborah, a medical receptionist, was due at work that morning.

"I put the kid to bed and cleaned up the breakfast dishes," he says. "I was off that day. I was sitting in the family room, and the phone rang. It was her office asking if she was coming in. I said, 'What do you mean, is she coming in?' They said she wasn't there, and my natural assumption was that the car broke down. It just didn't hit me what was going on. Then several hours passed, and she didn't call, didn't show up. I called the police. I called the hospitals, her parents, even the jail. Nobody had seen or heard from her."

Six days later, on July 4, they found Deborah's body in the trunk of the Plymouth—mutilated and decomposing where the car had been abandoned. "It was like a straight right to the face," says Groseclose. "There for about two or three minutes, it just wasn't real. Even after the funeral, it was just a void, empty, like now what?"

Prosecutors for the State of Tennessee tell the story differently. They say that Groseclose, working through a young intermediary named Barton Wayne Mount, hired two men to kill his wife—paying Phillip Britt and Ronald Rickman $100 apiece so that he could collect on a $32,000 insurance policy.

The prosecution case is based largely on the testimony of Mount, who, in return for his account of the crime, plea-bargained a sentence of ten years in prison. Britt also confessed and was sentenced to life. Rickman, a South Carolinian whose failed ambition was to join a motorcycle gang, admitted that he and Britt kidnapped Deborah Groseclose, but said she was still alive when they left her.

He was sentenced to death.

For a time, Rickman and Groseclose were compelled to share a cell. But they fought, and the arrangement was altered. Today, Groseclose is three cells away, living with one of two realities: Either he is guilty of a monstrous act of violence, a brutal aberration from his life before and after, or he is innocent—facing death because of the murder of a woman he once loved, living in proximity to a man who may have killed her.

"It's a crazy situation," says Harmon Wray, a Nashville minister who has visited Groseclose regularly over the past five years. "It's remarkable, really, that he has managed to stay sane. He's serious about his faith. He studied the Bible and was ordained as a minister after his conviction. I think that and his sense of humor have kept him together."

Wray says he is uncertain about Groseclose's future. He hopes for the best from the appeals process, now half completed. But he believes that if it fails, Groseclose will die. Because of the horror of the crime, and because members of Deborah Groseclose's family are calling in their grief for rapid executions, Wray says no governor of Tennessee would be inclined to commute the sentence.

In January of 1982, Groseclose came within four days of his execution date. He became increasingly morose as the time drew near, more cynical and self-pitying, and it had an effect on the morale of the row. Even the guards became gloomy, and when the word finally arrived that Groseclose had gotten a stay, one of them—a burly black veteran of the prison force—hurried in with the news. "Hey, Groseclose," he said, "we're glad you're gonna stick around."

"Bill's style really does have an effect on people," says Jeff Blum, a staff member with the anti-capital punishment Southern Prison Ministry. "He plays the role of mediator. He's a leader, pretty up most of the time, someone who is in control of his situation. He is not an extraordinary person. He has his ego and his foibles; he's very ordinary. But in his circumstances, that's not an easy thing to be."

For his own part, Groseclose is fatalistic. "This whole thing has endowed me with a lot of patience," he says. "If you are truly going to let the Lord lead you, if it's his wish that I burn in that chair, I will. Death is just a doorway.

"But when I think about all the things I've learned and thought about, all I've grown, all the listening I've done, I just can't imagine wasting all that for five cents of electricity."

CHAPTER 14

The Extravagant, Childlike Faith
of Jim Bakker

For reasons that have more to do with chance than anything else, Charlotte, N.C., has emerged over the years as one of America's home bases for mass market evangelism. It is the birthplace of Billy Graham and the headquarters for evangelist Jim Bakker and his PTL Television Network. The next two chapters profile Bakker and Graham—examining the excessive and childlike faith of one of them, the newfound and reflective maturity of the other.

November, 1981

It was an ordinary day at the PTL Club. There, against a backdrop of glittery stage lights—reds, blues and assorted shades of yellow—was Henry Harrison, a large-nosed man, pudgy and gray-suited, with a resolute smile of oblivious good cheer.

Harrison is the Ed McMahon of Christian television—amiable, un-threatening, full of hallelujahs and other bursts of enthusiasm. He is a perfect straightman for evangelist Jim Bakker, who, more than 20 years ago, fled his working class origins in Muskegon Heights, Mich., hitting the road for Jesus in a dusty white Valiant.

For the past 15 years, Bakker has been a talk show host, an evangelical's Johnny Carson, pouring forth his testimonials in Virginia and California and now, most recently, from the outskirts of Charlotte. He is bright and ambitious, a pioneer in the field of Christian communications. He is gifted with words and as cool as his medium, facile and unflappable when the stage lights are on.

At 41, Bakker seems to be sincere in his commitment to Christianity, but he is also insecure—embroiled perpetually in a swirl of controversy, an Elmer Gantry extravagance that has driven his national Christian network to the dizzy edge of ruin.

So there is Henry Harrison on Labor Day weekend, flashing another smile, the sweat beads visible on his stage make-up. He draws himself up tall before the red light of a camera, and he exhorts a million viewers with a disc jockey's resonance: "If you can't give $1,000, give

$500. Whatever you can do, we need to hear from you. The important thing is that you do it today."

Harrison's pleas came a year to the day after a PTL celebration—Victory Day, Jim Bakker had called it—with parades and preaching and 40,000 people, who had gathered then to proclaim PTL's new stability, a financial sobriety that Bakker avowed would last. But it didn't. Before a year had passed, PTL was $13 million behind on its bills—a crisis of the sort that Bakker seems to need.

He revels in his battles with impending catastrophe—sparring with reporters and federal investigators, gnashing his way through estrangements from his wife. All of it sends him through roller-coaster mood swings, from self-congratulation to self-pity, and most of it is played before his television audience—mixing strangely, somehow, with his professions of faith.

He will stride onstage to the rolling of drums, a short and smiling man of 5-feet-6, with his snugly tailored suit and a Bible in his hand. Then he will reach for his mike and proclaim with a sudden shout, his high-pitched voice filled with righteous conviction: "I believe God wants us to have victory! I believe he wants you to have victory! If you are a born-again Christian, you are going to triumph; you are going to win. I believe even if you are going through a valley, if you commit it to God, he will bring a victory in your life.

"We're so glad so many people have come to be a part of what is going on and help us see victory at PTL. You know, Oral Roberts mentioned to his own staff, 'We're going to take an offering for PTL.' And Richard Roberts, that's Oral's son, said that crowd stood to its feet and gave a standing ovation that they were going to give an offering to PTL.

"Five members of Rex Humbard's staff sat there and prayed for me every day for a week . . . God sent friends . . . I thought I had died and gone to heaven."

It soon became clear in the course of such monologues that Bakker is selling at least two things. One is certainly his understanding of faith—the efficacy and practicality of a relationship with God. But the other, simply put, is PTL—which is as much a monument to Bakker as it is to the Gospel.

And yet for all of that, there is something about him—some odd, guileless quality of childlike belief, some kernel of pure faith that you can't quite dismiss. It stirs the devotion of the millions who follow him, and reminds even certain cynics of a quotation from William Faulkner, delivered in the dialect of one of his characters:

"I reckin I've knowed de Lawd to use curiouser tools than this."

Bakker was born in 1940, the youngest of four children of working

class parents. He was small and insecure, weighing, as his parents now remember it, only 28 pounds when he began the first grade. He was terrified as he walked toward the school grounds, and things didn't improve as his early years unfolded.

He was shy, unathletic and a terrible student, and he was embarrassed by the modest circumstances of his family. "My father's name was Raleigh Bakker," he writes in his autobiography. "He worked as a machinist in a piston-ring factory and made a decent living. But I thought we lived in poverty.

"I was even embarrassed about my family's house. A cement-block structure in Muskegon Heights, the house had been painted what Daddy thought would be a buff-colored paint. It turned out to be orange! Whenever someone drove me home from school, I'd ask to be dropped off several blocks away so they wouldn't see the house.

"It seemed like anything I had was inferior to what other kids had. Year after year, I wore the same tattered blue baseball jacket with prominent white stitching, until the stitching unraveled completely.

"From the orange house to my dilapidated jacket to my poor school grades, I became filled with deep-seated feelings of inferiority."

The feelings have never left him, but he seems to have found relief in the glitter and applause, the accolades and visibility, from his life as a performer. He began as a DJ, spinning rock 'n' roll records for his high school sock hops. But he soon graduated to the heady world of preaching, spending a couple of years at a Minnesota Bible college, then dropping out to marry his sweetheart, Tammy LaValley.

Together, they launched a career as itinerant evangelists, preaching their earliest crusades in the mill town churches of North Carolina. From the beginning, his message showed traces of compassion—flashes of pained identification with the plight of underdogs. But mostly he seemed obsessed with numbers and results—with the streams of weeping people surging forward at the altar calls. And when it didn't happen, he was invariably distraught.

"I preached my heart out," he said of one early service, "gave the altar call . . . and nothing happened. I couldn't believe it! Instead of people streaming to the altar, the congregation just sat back staring at me. After the service, I walked back to the pastor's office feeling like the end of the world had come. I got down on my knees and sobbed my heart out into the green carpet . . . I was a failure."

That particular episode occurred nearly 20 years ago, and although Bakker still has his problems with rejection, still is given to self-absorption and despair, failure doesn't confront him as often anymore. He is skillful at his craft, developing a theology of runaway optimism—assuring his followers with an ear-to-ear grin and an earnest jab of his index finger that "God loves you—he really does."

The reflections of that love, Bakker argues, are apparent in every conceivable aspect of life. For those who believe, God will cause ulcers to heal, high blood pressure to subside and marital problems to change into harmony. He will cause cancers to disappear, prodigal sons and daughters to turn from their sins and financial worries to vanish in the night.

There is, in fact, no problem too trivial or material to escape the Lord's attention. During a PTL installment a couple of years ago, Bakker told the story of a Midwestern family who had written to say they had been praying for a Winnebago camper, but couldn't afford one. Finally, the family members reported, the Lord delivered a financial windfall, and they managed to buy a Winnebago in precisely the shade of brown that they had been seeking.

"Praise God," affirmed Bakker as the testimonial was read. "And if you pray for a camper, tell God what color."

Such is Bakker's understanding of faith—a sort of theology of payoffs in return for true belief. There are those who argue, of course, that it bears a disconcerting similarity to the old Janis Joplin song: "Oh Lord, won't you buy me a Mercedes-Benz. My friends all drive Porsches, I must make amends."

But it seems to appeal to the masses who have watched him, ever since Nov. 28, 1966, when he began a Christian talk show in Portsmouth, Va. His mentor in those days was Pat Robertson, a handsome, aristocratic Virginian, who had heard the call of the Lord a few years earlier and launched a television enterprise called the Christian Broadcasting Network.

Robertson was impressed with Bakker's eager preaching, his flamboyant and childlike absorption with Jesus. But he was occasionally put off by Bakker's ambition—a petulance, competitiveness and fragile ego that made him difficult to work with as a talk show co-host. And although Bakker's seven years at CBN were successful and fulfilling, Robertson was at least a little relieved when Bakker decided to move on—searching for a new network and a number one billing.

Bakker soon found both in California. He moved to Los Angeles in 1972 and went to work at a Christian enterprise called Trinity Broadcasting. He lasted a little more than a year, then quit in a dispute with the network's executives—splitting the staff and taking about half of them with him when he moved from there to Charlotte.

Upon his arrival in North Carolina, he took over as host of an amateurish talk show called "Praise The Lord." He changed the name to PTL on the theory that an enigmatic title wouldn't offend nonbelievers, and he set about creating his own network. Success came quickly. By the mid-'70s, PTL was seen daily in more than 200 cities, and contributions were flowing in at the rate of $1 million a week. Today the hour-long talk show reaches about a million viewers a day, independent rating services estimate, and draws $3.5 million a month in contributions.

Bakker suddenly found himself with an international following, legions of troubled, searching people who were caught up in his charisma. But along with the successes, there have been major problems—financial catastrophes and administrative chaos and a nagging, two-year investigation by the federal government.

It soon becomes clear that the problems are related, springing from Bakker's preoccupation with his status, his fascination with the glittery trappings of acclaim. Ever since his boyhood—the days of his tattered jacket, orange house and bad grades in school—he has been consumed by anxiety over his standing in the world. In the startling candor of his autobiography, he writes of the beginnings of his climb toward success:

"We never told anyone our apartment didn't have a bedroom. With so many doors opening off the huge living room, everybody thought the door leading to the furnace was our bedroom. We purchased a comfortable hide-a-bed and that worked out fine until God could perform another miracle with accommodations.

"One day Tammy was taking the elevator up to our apartment. 'And what floor do you live on?' a society matron asked with her nose pointed high in the air.

" 'The seventh,' Tammy hung her head slightly.

" 'We live on the 18th,' the woman said tartly.

"The 18th floor was the most expensive in the high-rise. We were perfectly satisfied with our efficiency on the seventh floor, but within a year, God had changed our financial situation so radically that we were able to move to the 18th floor ourselves.

"Then when the society matrons would ask Tammy, 'And what floor do you live on?' she could say, "Praise God, we've gone to 18.' "

Such social climbing may seem peculiar for someone who believes, as Bakker professes he does, that the end of the world is rapidly approaching—that within a few years there will be a final rapture, a sudden plucking of Christians from their earthly surroundings into a blissful, eternal proximity with God.

But such are the contradictions of Bakker's personality, the gaps between his theology and the impulses of his psyche. And at PTL, the gaps have grown wider. He has lived in seven houses in the past six years, moving when it suits him—most recently to a $350,000 lakeside estate, purchased by his ministry even as its debts had soared into the millions.

Earlier this year, he and his wife were driving a fleet of five cars, including a Rolls Royce, a Thunderbird, a Continental and a Fiat, all of them furnished by PTL. In the midst of a similar financial crisis a couple of years ago, he made a tearful, televised plea for money—announcing that he and Tammy "are giving every penny of our life savings to PTL." Less than a month later, he spent $6,000 as a down-payment on a houseboat.

Not all of that, however, is Bakker himself. Much of it is Tammy, his wife and featured gospel singer on PTL, renowned for spending sprees at Charlotte's shopping malls. She was demure and plain when Bakker met and married her 20 years ago. But she's developed a weakness these days for lacy black dresses with startling plunges at the neck and heavy coats of makeup applied in the mornings (a liquid beige base, she explains, with dark V's of contour powder to accentuate her cheeks).

Bakker is not entirely happy with his wife's latest look, and it is not the first time there have been differences between them. In 1970, for example, after the first of their two children was born in Virginia, Tammy went into a depression ("I was a zombie," she said, "for about a year"). She became so distant that Bakker considered separation. "She didn't want a physical relationship," he explained. "That is bound to offend any man."

But they managed to pray their way through it, and although they have had upheavals since then—including at least one leave-taking by Tammy—they are still together and intermittently happy, driving fancy cars, redecorating houses and traveling around the world on missions for the Lord.

But the Bakkers' personal extravagance is not the central cause for PTL's money problems. The organization's difficulties grew out of Bakker's decision—on orders from God, he insisted—to build a $100 million Total Living Center near the outskirts of Charlotte. It didn't take long for the project to consume him. He would sometimes awaken at 3 a.m., fumbling through the dark for a sheet of legal paper, sketching out the plans for still another building. It might be an auditorium in the shape of a barn or a tiered office building that would look like a pyramid.

Most days would find him at the construction site, choking cheerfully on the Caterpillar dust or slogging along gamely through the ankle-deep mud. He envisioned campgrounds, ballparks and condominiums for the elderly; office buildings, studios and a massive amphitheater.

But when the bills poured in, he simply couldn't pay them. He developed a reputation for misleading his creditors, and at one point in the middle of the ordeal, he raised more than $300,000 for an overseas missions project—then spent it on PTL's mounting debts.

Such extravagance and deception generated bad press—critical articles in a variety of publications—and a two-year investigation by the

*The pyramid-shaped building and church
are part of PTL's Heritage Village, a
Christian retreat 15 miles south of Charlotte, N.C.*

Federal Communications Commission. The investigation is not yet complete. But during the course of it, Bakker has fought back in a couple of ways.

First, he paid more than $300,000 to an overseas missions project that was similar to the one for which he had originally raised the money. And he argued that the first project had been fraught with problems anyway.

But mostly what he did was lash out publicly. Buoyed by the crowds at the tapings of his show, he would gaze at the camera with a sad-eyed expression, looking for all the world like a wounded little boy. Sometimes he would cry, and sometimes he would merely choke on the emotion of the words:

"I believe," he declared, "if we were forced off the air it will be the saddest day in the history of the nation. It's a sad, sad thing, but you are guilty until proven innocent. There is no wrongdoing at PTL. There are the lies that have been written about us. The lies have been propagated by the enemies of the ministry. . . . It's a conspiracy. I've watched it for months."

To the people who didn't like him, such statements had the ring of paranoia. But there was more to it than that. There was theology involved—a kind of Onward-Christian-Soldier understanding of the world, a vision of God's people at war with non-believers.

"The forces of Satan," he would write later, "are drawing together to make a last stand against the cause of Christ. But God's spirit is raising up a mighty standard to defeat Satan, and that standard is the church. If the church is going to defeat Satan, if the church is going to survive the attack of the ages, then the church must unite—she must unite to live."

The church, Bakker argued, is the body of believers—a powerful Christian army with an elite corps of generals: Pat Robertson, Billy Graham, Oral Roberts, Rex Humbard. And of course, Jim Bakker. So it follows, he reasoned, "when Jim Bakker is having a problem and is called before government, that is Christianity being called before the government."

For a time, starting in 1979, Bakker dabbled in an alliance of evangelical generals—a fledgling coalition including Pat Robertson, Jerry Falwell and James Robison of Fort Worth, Tex. Later it became the Falwell-dominated Moral Majority. But in the beginning, it was more informal than that—a fantasy, really, of evangelical Christians marching toward the polls, seizing the reins of political power and using them to pursue a great moral revival.

They would ban abortions and defeat the Equal Rights Amendment, beef up the military for the struggle against Communism and find some way to put prayer back in schools. They would do battle with pornography and homosexuality and fire the anti-Christian bureaucrats at the FCC. Jim Bakker didn't agree with all of that, but he found it, nevertheless, a goose-pimply fantasy—mighty legions of Jesus people in pursuit of God's agenda, rising to victory over the counter-attacks of Satan.

But then something stopped him. It was difficult at first to understand what snapped, to fathom the queasiness and misgivings that began to beset him. But it was all very simple, and more than a little surprising to the critics who wrote him off. In theological terms, Bakker had pursued his Christian Soldier understandings to their logical extension—to a political militance on the world's own turf. But somehow, it seemed, the crusade had turned sour, had taken on a nastiness that he simply didn't share.

He was put off by James Robison's bitter tirades on homosexuality, by Jerry Falwell's hostility to racial integration. And he wanted to hear somebody talk about the hungry.

Despite his petulance and his yearning for martyrdom, Bakker also has an instinct for compassion—almost in spite of himself, a deep-seated affinity for the gentle side of the Christian message. He is given to frequent quotings of the Sermon on the Mount, and of the social-gospel passages that are scattered through Luke.

It is more than a matter of theatrics when he closes his eyes and lets his voice drop low, lets it tremble slightly as he begins to talk to God: "I'll pray today for those who are hurting. I pray for those who are in pain. I pray for the poor and those who want to give up. I pray for that one who wants to commit suicide. Help him to know that you have promised victory."

He is even more expansive in the privacy of his office, in the padded spacious reaches behind his hardwood desk, lounging there in his open-necked shirt, with a gold-chained medallion dangling at his chest. He speaks softly and with an air of reflection, and it is very hard to imagine that he doesn't mean what he says:

"You know, a lot of people think we preach Utopia, that everything is going to be right if you accept Christ. That's not true. Christians are not perfect. As the bumper sticker says, they're just forgiven. We have problems, but we have a God, and the God I have come to know personally is a compassionate, loving savior who cares for people.

"In our Sunday school department when I was a boy, we had a picture of this eye about six feet wide, and it said, 'This eye is watching you, you, you.' So we sang this little song that said, 'Be careful little eye what you see; be careful little feet where you go.' We had this image that God had this big club, and if we stepped out of boundaries, He was going to bash us. That's not the God I know, because of course we step out of boundaries all the time, and still He loves us.

"You know, people ask me how I feel about certain things. They ask how I feel about the role of women, and I say I feel that what's happening in the world is parallel to what's happening in the church. There's good in the women's liberation movement in this country today. There's so much good that it's about 95 percent good. I think God is trying to get us to elevate the place of women . . . and I feel about women in the ministry the same way I do about black and white. I really don't see black and white. We're seeing the move of God's spirit bringing us together.

"Or maybe someone will ask about capital punishment, and I say I guess I'm against it because I couldn't pull the switch. Or about homosexuals: I say I think we ought to welcome them into our churches, because we're not going to reach the homosexual for Christ by segregating them off to one side and preaching hate."

So Bakker didn't fit with the Moral Majority. His agenda and instincts were of an entirely different sort, and throughout 1980, he backed away increasingly from Falwell and his people. By the fall, in violation of his own philosophy of Christian solidarity, he took a mild, but explicit slap at Falwell's brand of politics— criticizing his open partisanship in support of Ronald Reagan.

"I don't think," Bakker announced, "that God is a Republican or a Democrat."

But in the end, Bakker's second thoughts about political militance among Christians began to go beyond his discomfort with Falwell. As one of his aides put it on the eve of the Presidential election, "The evangelical community almost seems to be saying, 'We don't want government having anything to do with us, but we do want to control the government.' That's not something we really ought to be saying, and I'm glad that Jim Bakker came to recognize the fact."

So how in the end do you make sense of Bakker?

Perhaps it helps to look back to Labor Day weekend of 1980, when 40,000 gathered at PTL, standing seven or eight deep along a two-mile parade route, clapping and shrieking as Bakker's float rumbled past. It was Victory Day, and the purpose of the occasion was to dedicate a building—a $2 million auditorium already paid for.

Oral Roberts was on hand to help celebrate, and he agreed to preach at the building's consecration. He chose his text from the Gospel of John—citing the story of a guileless little boy who trusted Jesus to feed the multitudes from a child's simple lunch. Bakker, said Roberts, has the same sort of faith—serving to remind us that "what Jesus needs is the little boy, and the little girl, in all of us."

Bakker's closest friends tend to see him that way, as a child at heart, but maybe also as a peculiar adolescent—caught in the crossfire of his competing inclinations.

He is petty, insecure, self-absorbed and materialistic—deeply entrapped by worldly measures of success. And yet, somehow, he is also decent—a sensitive, humane and self-effacing little man, who has developed an affinity for the compassion of Jesus.

This much, at least, is clear.

At Victory Day, a classic PTL occasion by Bakker's own admission, there was a crucial inappropriateness in Oral Roberts' analogy—his comparison of Bakker and the child in the Gospel. The Victory Day agenda was about as far removed as possible from the feeding of the hungry, which was what Jesus did in the story Roberts cited. Roberts, of course, was dedicating a building—celebrating Bakker's opening of a glistening auditorium. And auditoriums, you could argue, are precisely the sorts of shrines that Jesus never built.

CHAPTER 15

The Mellowing of Billy Graham

If Martin Luther King, with whom this book began, is the symbol of black American Christianity, his white counterpart has to be Billy Graham—perhaps the most famous Christian in the history of the faith. This profile focuses on how he has changed, the mellowing and expansion of his definition of Christianity. It was written before his controversial trip to Moscow, which occurred in May of 1982, but I have added an epilogue on the trip and its significance.

August, 1981

The stadium suddenly filled with the sound of his voice, rich and honey-toned and gently pleading, the words familiar after so many years, falling on the crowd of 32,000. His thoughts and phrases were mostly unremarkable, streams of certainty about the power of the faith, the disaster that looms at the end of other paths.

"You come forward now, men and women, black or white; you come, hundreds of you. It'll only take a moment to come. Mothers, fathers, young people too. The ushers will show you. You may be an elder or a deacon in the church, but you come. . . ."

And they did come, moving forward silently in numbers that were startling—some weeping softly, others holding hands and popping Juicy Fruit gum, but coming, streaming down the aisles from throughout the arena, the choir as always singing, "Just As I Am." And above it all the same hypnotic voice:

"You come now. . . . It's important that you come. There's something about coming forward and standing here that helps settle it in your mind. . . ."

When you see Billy Graham in that kind of setting—when he stands before the crowd with his sun-tanned face and his pale blue stare, with the odd, lingering innocence of some aging surfer—it's a little hard to fathom what it all really means. There is an air about him of absolute sincerity. But what about the substance? What are crowds left with when the service is over? What vision, what understanding of the depths of Christianity?

His critics have answered such questions harshly, contending over the years that there's a clunking banality at the heart of Graham's message, a sanitized, Americanized understanding of Jesus that renders him irrelevant to 20th-century turmoil.

Rheinhold Niebuhr was one of the first to make the charge. In the tumultuous summer of 1956—a time when Martin Luther King and his followers were boycotting buses in pursuit of integration—Niebuhr wrote an article for the Christian Century. He quoted the epistle of First John ("If a man sayeth he loves God and hateth his brother, he is a liar") and urged Graham to speak out about racial upheavals.

Other critics emerged in the '60s and '70s, culminating in 1979, when journalist Marshall Frady produced a biography of Graham—an eloquent critique that drew wide acclaim. Frady concluded that Graham, the farmboy evangelist from the outskirts of Charlotte, was so affected by the wooings of the powerful that he could no longer distinguish between Richard Nixon's America and the Kingdom of God.

". . . It is no accident," wrote Frady, "that Graham has wound up now with his image translated into a stained-glass window in Washington's National Presbyterian Cathedral. He constitutes finally the apotheosis of the American Innocence itself—that plain, cheerful, rigorous, ferociously wholesome earnestness which, to some, as one Egyptian editor put it during the days of Vietnam, 'has made you nice Americans the most dangerous people on the face of the earth.' "

But two years later, the criticism is fading. There is a widespread feeling that Graham has mellowed, almost suddenly and strangely, and that his thinking has taken on at least a faint prophetic tinge. He speaks out now on a host of social issues, from hunger to nuclear weapons, declaring during a recent crusade in Baltimore:

"We are staring at the possibility of war in the Middle East, or an invasion of Poland. We are spending a million dollars a minute on armaments all over the world, little nations working on the atomic bomb. . . . People are hungry and starving in Somalia and other places. . . . Have we gone mad? . . . Are we seeking the genocide of the whole human race?"

"I've developed a great admiration for Billy Graham," says Rabbi Marc Tannenbaum, a liberal Jewish leader who has talked often with Graham. "Just look at him today and the way that he's grown." And even Marshall Frady now admits a little warily: "I think he's changed. I really do believe it."

So the question becomes, are Tannenbaum and Frady really right? Or is Graham, as people often are, still far more complex than anyone's summary of him?

The first time I met him, I did not expect to like him.

It was a misty June Sunday in 1979, a couple of months after the appearance of Frady's book. Graham meandered into the living room of his spacious log home, hidden away on a mountain in the town of Montreat. He moved with a slouching, good-natured gait, his arms dangling loosely at his side, and he seemed very different from his TV persona—vastly more vulnerable and even a little shy.

My awareness of him had crystalized during bursts of public certitude, in the heat of the '60s, amid all the national agony over Vietnam. He would pound at the pulpits on television crusades, inveighing against the storms of youthful rebellion. "There is just too much negativism," he would say in those days. "There are too many people knocking our institutions. . . ." And he would call to the podium assorted young Marines, clean-cut and earnest, to explain how God had helped them kill Communists.

On domestic moral issues, he was equally as shrill. In 1971, for example, in his hometown of Charlotte, all the city's powerful gathered in his honor—on an unseasonably hot October afternoon, with a private reception featuring Danish lobster tails and cross-shaped sandwiches and a 30-pound cake in the shape of a Bible. There was also a public ceremony with 12,000 people, during which he offered inflated recollections of his boyhood hardships:

"We also wrestled with poverty, if you go by today's standards, except we did not know we were poor. We did not have sociologists, educators and newscasters constantly reminding us of how poor we were." Then he added to the applause of the crowd: "We also had the problem of rats. The only difference between then and now is we didn't call upon the federal government to kill them. . . ."

But eight years later in the summer of '79—in the reassuring privacy of a drizzly afternoon—his tone sounded different. He sank back leisurely on a padded couch and discussed the social implications of the Christian Gospel. As the conversation bounced from topic to topic—from nuclear war and hunger to capital punishment—he revealed some instincts that hadn't been apparent.

He was troubled, he said, by the resumption of capital punishment, the taint it could inflict on American justice.

"I just don't know," he explained. "We live in a time of horrible and hideous crimes. But one of the hesitations I've always had is that so many more blacks are executed. The system has always been too one-sided, and many of the people on death row are poor people who couldn't afford good lawyers.

"There is no perfect system of justice on this earth. God will have it at the judgment. But this is a very imperfect system. And execution makes the imperfection final."

But then he added in an odd little demurral: "Of course, I have never taken a stand on capital punishment. . . . I have to be careful what I say about a great many things."

Such hedgings have always been characteristic of Graham. Even in the cloister of his Montreat home, with its flock of friendly dogs and expansive hearth of old-fashioned brick, he seems inescapably aware that he is an institution. His identity is tied to his sense of mission, and he will let nothing—absolutely nothing—jeopardize his calling.

"My main focus is the Gospel," he explains with some urgency, as if it matters a great deal that his visitor understand. "I'm concerned about what it can do for you, for a person's life. There may be issues distantly related to the Gospel, or perhaps they are deeply related. But the gift of an evangelist is a very narrow gift."

His awareness of that gift has defined his life—ever since his sixteenth year, when, as a handsome, thoroughly ordinary teenager, given to mischievous transgressions regarding girls and fast cars, he and a buddy decided to take in a revival in Charlotte.

They winced at the ferocity of the presiding evangelist—an itinerant, florid-faced anti-Semite named Mordecai Ham—but they moved forward tremulously at the altar-call. Graham says today that he almost didn't go. But at the last possible moment, with an ill-defined guilt surging violently inside him, he walked hesitantly up the aisle and asked Jesus to forgive him.

The experience left him with an exalted sense of propriety, a tendency to scold his friends for the most minor misbehavior— and before long you could find him on Charlotte street-corners, stalking and raging and preaching to pedestrians, charging them to repent before it was too late.

A year and a half later, in 1936, he and a friend, Grady Wilson, graduated from high school and set off to South Carolina for a summer of traveling, selling Fuller brushes and witnessing for Jesus when the opportunity arose. Then he went away to college—first to the hard-bitten, ultra-fundamentalist Bob Jones University, where he was miserable, then on to the more warm-hearted Florida Bible Institute.

There, in the suburbs of Tampa, his thinking and style took on the first hints of polish. His faith seemed to deepen. His fire and brimstone understanding of sin became at least a little tempered by his sunny disposition, his gathering optimism about the effectiveness of faith.

And after graduation, as his evangelizing gained momentum in the 1940s, the crowds were caught up in his natural, vibrant decency. He still lunged about the pulpit and lashed at the air with his pointed forefinger—still warned them urgently of the ravages of hell. But there was an undeniable compassion about him, then as now, when he stood before the people at the altar invitation, and told them softly:

"I have no power to save anybody, to forgive anybody, to heal anybody. . . . I'm praying right now while I'm talking to you. I'm praying, 'Lord, help me say the right thing to that person before me. . . ."

But there was another major component to Graham's appeal —one that caught the attention of some powerful people and thrust him suddenly into superstardom. Not only did he embody all the traditional American virtues—"You slip down to the cocktail lounge and listen to those dirty, filthy stories, and you laugh, and you're just as guilty as if you told the story and committed the act. . . ."—he also saw America as God's great hope, a righteous instrument to evangelize the world.

During a Los Angeles crusade in 1949, he proclaimed that the planet "is divided into two camps. On the one side we see Communism. On the other, we see so-called Western culture, with its fruit and its foundation in the Bible, the Word of God, and in the revivals of the seventeenth and eighteenth centuries. Communism, on the other hand, has declared war against God, against Christ, against the Bible. . . ."

Such words fell pleasantly on the ears of William Randolph Hearst, the irascible West Coast newspaper magnate. "And that was when," explains Grady Wilson, Graham's associate evangelist for more than 30 years, "Mr. Hearst gave the order to 'puff Graham.' "

What Mr. Hearst ordered his reporters quickly did, and suddenly Graham's picture was splattered across the pages of the nation's biggest papers—prompting soon afterwards Time-Life's Henry Luce to get into the act. And as Wilson remembers it, "Mr. Luce ran a three-page color spread and story. . . ."

Graham was stunned, perhaps even frightened, by the sudden and unrelenting gales of attention. He remembers that he telephoned a colleague in Chicago and told him: "You better get out here. Something's happening, and I don't know what it is. It's way beyond me."

Such feelings of inadequacy are not at all surprising. Graham has about him a genuine, deep-rooted, almost awesome humility —a rigorous understanding of his own ordinariness—that's still intact after 30 years of accolades. It is, perhaps, his most touching trait. But it has a peculiar flip side—a lingering need to justify himself, which has left him, unfortunately, susceptible to flattery.

And the flattery has come from the highest of places—beginning with Hearst and Luce and spreading quickly into the realm of politics. After the Los Angeles crusade, Graham and his team moved on to Boston—"the closest thing to a real revival we've experienced," says Grady Wilson. There, amid the emotion of overflow crowds, they attracted the attention of House Speaker John McCormack—a Massachusetts Catholic, who was impressed by the effectiveness of Graham's appeal.

"He decided that Billy should meet President Truman," says Wilson.

So the visit was arranged—Graham, Wilson and a couple of other team members talking stiffly with Truman, then suddenly and exuberantly suggesting a prayer. Truman seemed somewhat embarrassed by it all, but such misgivings faded in the minds of his successors.

Eisenhower, Johnson and Richard Nixon—even the urbane John Kennedy—recognized the benefits of cordiality with Graham. They praised him publicly and courted him privately —Eisenhower calling him "the greatest ambassador that America has"—and Graham, for his part, returned the admiration.

"Nobody," says former Johnson aide and protege Bill Moyers, "could make Johnson feel he was right quite like Billy Graham could." And Johnson, of course, was in need of that, for like Nixon after him, he was presiding over a war and a national dissolution—the ungluing, as Moyers noted, of the veneer of consensus that held the country together.

It became clear in those bitter days—despite careful hedgings and disingenuous denials—that Graham had planted his feet on a particular side of the chasm. While insisting that he was neutral on the war, he poured forth an uncountable number of statements like these: U.S. troops "know why they are fighting in Vietnam, and they believe what they are doing is right. . . . We either face an all-out war with Red China or a retreat that will cause us to lose face throughout Asia . . ." And when Martin Luther King denounced the war, Graham called it "an affront to the thousands of loyal Negro troops who are in Vietnam."

His critics became numerous in the wake of such pronouncements. Protestors began showing up at his speeches, armed with placards denouncing his stands. Even other ministers began to criticize him harshly —and not just the Ivy League liberals, who believed that Jesus was a social reformer, but also a growing number of evangelicals.

Chief among the latter were a pair of clerics, Jim Holloway and Will Campbell, who headed a loosely-knit Christian confederation called the Committee of Southern Churchmen. Holloway was a teacher at Berea College in Kentucky, Campbell a Southern Baptist expatriate from Mississippi, a renegade preacher who had been deeply involved in the civil rights movement.

In 1971, during the peak years of friendship between Graham and Richard Nixon, Campbell and Holloway wrote an open letter, published in a religious journal called Katallagete. They urged Graham to take a cue from the Old Testament prophets and to use his influence to lobby for peace: ". . . Why do we address ourselves to you, Dr. Graham? . . . We believe the only way you, or any of us, can *minister* to the White House or the Pentagon is to *prophesy* to the White House and the Pentagon in the tradition of Micaiah, son of Imlah. And you, our brother, have been and will be the prophet summoned to those halls. We shall not."

Graham generally responded to the criticism pleasantly. "I want you to know," he wrote Campbell and Holloway, "that I do not take it personally and am not the slightest bit offended. Sometime we might be able to sit down privately and discuss the points you have raised. . . ." But that was it. The meeting didn't happen, for Graham simply resubmerged—with a kind of gee-whiz overflow of modesty and gratitude—into the stream of acclamation that came his way.

"All this for a preacher—and an evangelist at that," he beamed in 1971, when 12,000 people, including Richard Nixon, turned out in Charlotte for a day in his honor. "I'm sure," he added graciously, when asked about the crowds, "they're coming to see the President, not me. . . ."

But then suddenly, it was gone. Nixon resigned in the throes of scandal, and Graham—who had supported him with more ardor and affection than he had ever felt for a political figure—found his own reputation in a severe state of taint. He was bewildered. He listened to the tapes, with all the vulgarities and sinister plottings, and two years later, he told Marshall Frady:

"I just couldn't understand it. I still can't. I thought he was a man of integrity, I looked upon him as the possibility of leading this country to its greatest and best days. And all those people around him, they seemed so clean, family men, so clean-living. Sometimes, when I look back on it all now, it has the aspects of a nightmare. . . ."

In the wake of that experience that brought him up short, confronting him starkly with the complexities of human nature, the evil that can lurk beneath benign exteriors, Graham has emerged as a more reflective person. He has absorbed a variety of thought-provoking experiences, and his relationship to American politics and culture—his understanding of America's mission in the world—is not what it was.

It would be easy and tempting to overstate the change. But you cannot *deny* it—not if you sit down with him on a shadowy afternoon, away from the pressures and demands of his massive organization, and listen to him talk about the things he now believes.

"I'm concerned," he will tell you, "about the terrifying weapons that are being developed at the moment, on all sides, the proliferation of nuclear arms. . . . Countries, especially in the Middle East, are working feverishly on the atomic bomb, and one of them could easily push a button and unleash an atomic war in the Middle East which could draw the whole world into it. . . .

"I feel that the Scriptures teach that not only are we to be peacemakers—the Scriptures say that we are to work hard at peace and live peaceably with all men. . . . I am not for unilateral disarmament. I think we have a right to defend ourselves . . . but I do feel that as human beings on a planet that can self-destruct we ought to sit down and say, 'Here, we must negotiate this.'

"I've said on occasion, I'm for Salt X, by which I mean the destruction of all nuclear weapons. But now yesterday, I believe, the Senate or some committee in the Senate passed a law or resolution that we go ahead and develop nerve gas. Sen. Hatfield strongly opposed it and wondered how far this madness was going to go. I feel the same way. And I look on it as a total Christian moral responsibility to speak out on it just as I would speak out on, say, the race question. . . ."

He continues to talk, acknowledging freely the things he doesn't know, the mistakes he has made, the regrets about his past and his lapses of wisdom.

"There are issues," he admits, "that I don't know the answer to. I don't know the answer to when a fetus becomes a person. . . . I don't think any of us really knows. There are people that think they do, but I don't. There are areas like this on which I'm not qualified to speak. . . . So I would say that in that sense there has been a pilgrimage in my thinking over a period of years that has accelerated maybe in the last five years. . . .

"My gospel hasn't changed, but the application of the gospel in social and political areas has changed . . . I might have been influenced by my trips to Eastern Europe where I saw vast groups of people who are praying and hoping for peace. In Poland, Hungary and other parts of the world, where everytime there is a war in Europe they seemed to be trampled on by either side.

"You know, Eisenhower once said publicly that I was the greatest ambassador that America had. . . . Of course at that moment when he said it in the 1950s, I was pleased. Now I would not be pleased because I feel that my ministry today is a world ministry. I think now when I say something, 'How is this going to sound in India? How is it going to sound to my friends in Hungary or Poland?'

"I don't ever want to dodge the truth, and I don't ever want to back down on what my convictions are. But I'm beginning to see that there are more sides to some of these questions than I once thought. I am not as dogmatic."

And so he is not. He seems fascinated now by his critics of the past—theologians like Rheinhold Niebuhr and Martin Marty, evangelical gadflies like Holloway and Campbell. On a recent trip to Nashville, he made it a point to get together with Campbell: "Just a brief meeting," he says. "But I liked him very much. I hope to get an appointment with him and go visit his farm, just sit down and talk for an afternoon."

There seems little doubt that the impulse is genuine. For Graham has, as one religion editor recently noted, "a capacity to chew on criticism and then learn something from it."

But in addition to the criticism—as well as the travel, disappointments and all the other factors that have shaped his thinking, Graham has been peculiarly influenced by another development: the sudden political militance among right-wing Christians. It has coalesced now into the Moral Majority. But it began with separate stirrings in Lynchburg, Norfolk, Charlotte and Fort Worth—the All-American bases for TV evangelism.

By the middle 1970s, Jerry Falwell, Jim Bakker and a large number of others had amassed vast followings—legions of conservative, God-fearing Americans, many of whom were disturbed by the drift of the country. They were concerned about abortion, defense, the ERA, crime, homosexuals and prayer in the schools. And they apparently believed that no one was listening.

"It is time," affirmed James Robison, a swashbuckling evangelist from outside of Ft. Worth, "for Christians to develop a get-tough, activitist attitude—or we're through."

So Robison began meeting with Falwell, Bakker, Pat Robertson and other leaders, and his staff let it slip that Billy Graham was involved. But Graham was not. He was put off by something in the spirit of the group—some hint of meanness imbedded in the rhetoric; and perhaps he sensed as well an echo of himself, his own Cold War struttings of 30 years ago, reincarnated now in the Moral Majority agenda.

For whatever reason, Graham kept his distance. Privately, he urged evangelical leaders to stay out of politics—particularly right-wing politics—and eventually he acknowledged to Parade magazine: "It would disturb me if there was a wedding between religious fundamentalists and the political right. The hard right has no interest in religion except to manipulate it."

For all of that, Graham may have paid a price. As Parade noted, he is not America's "hot evangelist" anymore. His organization's annual budget of about $30 million is approximately half the yearly total raised by Falwell. His 1980 crusades—including a disastrously attended gathering in Nevada—drew fewer people than in any year since 1949. And his associate evangelist Grady Wilson admits: "I happen to know a lot of his friends have been disappointed in some of the things he's said. . . ."

Graham has never been one to enjoy disapproval. So you find him today occasionally doubling back, taking careful steps to cover his flank—writing Falwell, for example, after the Parade article appeared and telling him earnestly in the letter's first sentence, "Dear Jerry: I am deeply disturbed that there seems to be an attempt to drive a wedge between us."

The instinct for caution still lingers in him strongly, and never is it more apparent than in his most public moments—when he cranks up the machinery of his massive organization and stages a crusade on behalf of Jesus Christ. . . .

In the bucolic green hills of western Maryland, out highway 40 from the bustle of Baltimore, Dale Aukerman raises strawberries with his wife and three children. He also writes—for Sojourners Magazine and other Christian publications—and most recently he completed a book called *Darkening Valley*: a radical Christian analysis of national defense.

He has studied Graham carefully for the last several years, and on a couple of levels, he admires him deeply. For one thing, Aukerman is an evangelical—a soft-spoken, 50-year-old believer in Jesus whose most urgent priority is to witness for the faith. He also respects Graham's stands on peace, and on March 13, 1981, he wrote to Graham at his home in Montreat:

"Our prayers will be with you as you come to Baltimore (for a crusade). We hope that many will be brought under the Lordship of Jesus through that week. We write particularly to tell you that a group of us have felt a leading to pass out fliers at some of the sessions. . . . Our concern is to call Christians away from the delusions of a nuclear arms race . . . to faithfulness in Jesus Christ. . . . We hope that you and your organization in Baltimore will see us as evangelical Christians sharing a crucial part of Christ's call to discipleship. . . ."

Graham was out of town when the letter arrived, and he didn't answer it. So Aukerman wrote several others—each time expressing support for Graham and his impending crusade, praising Graham's stand on nuclear weapons and explaining that he and a handful of members of his denomination, the Church of the Brethren, simply wanted to offer a public witness for their faith.

On May 26, he received a reply from a Graham aide, crusade director Elwyn Cutler, who informed him with bureaucratic politeness that fliers for peace would not be allowed.

"I find the general feeling on the executive committee to be in harmony with the established policy that governs all of our crusades," Cutler said. "That policy is to the effect that only Billy Graham materials are allowed to be distributed before, during or following a crusade service. . . . We have many and all kinds of requests to allow distribution of material. To give permission in one case and not in another is a very difficult posture for us."

It soon became clear that Cutler meant what he said. On June 9, the night after Graham had denounced nuclear weapons from the crusade podium, Aukerman and perhaps a dozen followers arrived at the public sidewalks and parking lots outside the stadium and began passing out anti-nuclear fliers—each of which began with a quote from Graham: "Is a nuclear holocaust inevitable if the arms race is not stopped? Frankly, the answer is almost certainly yes."

They made no attempt to enter the stadium, but their presence outside so enraged crusade officials that several men with usher's badges began shouting at Aukerman—"Why are you trying to spread this poison!"—and after shoving a minister who was with him, they summoned Baltimore police to force him to leave.

Aukerman saw it as an irony of institutional religion—a collision between the gospel and crusade policy. From throughout Baltimore, more than 9,000 people were participating directly in crusade activities; there were 1,500 ushers, 2,500 counselors, 4,000 people singing in the choir. But a dozen people witnessing for peace—even when they were passing out quotes from Graham himself—were perceived as a threat that had to be removed.

After more than 270 crusades across the world, however, the Graham staff has developed a formula for success. It does not include endorsement of any other causes—or radical interpretations of what the gospel means.

"The key is involvement," says Sterling Houston, a tall and primly affable man who is Graham's director of North American crusades. "There are two important principles of crusade organization . . . the human dynamic and the spiritual dynamic."

Basically, the Graham staff spends about a year with local volunteers, who in turn recruit as many people as they can—choir members, ushers and all the rest. They supplement their efforts with some serious praying, and over the years, the results have been stunning—crowds totalling more than 58 million.

It is, of course, the essence of what Graham does, and he is careful to do nothing to jeopardize the system. On other occasions, he will speak out strongly—calling for disarmament on the CBS Evening News, telling national religious broadcasters to be concerned for social justice, or to beware of the idolatry of money and success.

But in a crusade setting, he is cautious, even testy, at the barest hint of controversy. In Baltimore, for example, he carefully skirted questions on Reagan's defense build-ups or the ill-fated nomination of Ernest Lefever, as the administration's human rights watchdog. "That's too political," he said of Lefever. "I'm sorry. I do have some private thoughts. But I don't think I ought to express them now. . . ."

He may speak in generalities about threats to world peace or plead from the pulpit for greater racial harmony. But he also believes, as he has said many times, that "the gift of an evangelist is a very narrow gift." So mostly what he does is call people forward, standing before them with a voice strong and gentle:

"You come now. . . . It's important that you come. There's something about coming forward and standing here that helps settle it in your mind. . . ."

And whatever else it means or doesn't mean, whatever the effect on the people who come, it is a vocation and a calling that consumes him completely.

Epilogue, June 1982

On April 20, 1982, shortly before his controversial and in many ways ill-fated trip to Moscow, Billy Graham made a stop at Harvard and delivered one of the finest speeches in his lengthy career. Among other things, this is what he said:

"I would like to say some things informally about my own pilgrimage and my own witness. My basic commitment as a Christian has not changed, nor had my view of the gospel. But I've come to see in deeper ways some of the implications of my faith and the message I've been proclaiming.

"I was born and reared on a small farm in Southern America. It rarely occurred to me in my childhood to think about the difficulties, problems and oppressions of black people. In high school, I began to question some of the practices, but it was not until I'd actually committed my life to Christ that I began to realize that if I were a Christian, I had to take a stand on the race question.

"I did not know how. But in 1952, I was holding a series of meetings in a Southern city. They had ropes so that black people had to sit behind those ropes. I went down and personally and physically pulled the ropes down. That was among my first acts of conscience on the race question . . .

"I often spoke on the wonderful little story in the tenth chapter of Luke where Jesus told the story of the good Samaritan, teaching us our social responsibilities. From the very beginning, I felt that if I came upon a person who had been beaten and robbed and left for dead that I'd do my best to help him. I also felt that this applied to my relatives and friends and immediate neighbors.

"But I never thought of it in terms of corporate responsibility. I had no real idea that millions of people throughout the world lived on the knife-edge of starvation and that the teachings of my reference point demanded that I have a responsibility toward them.

"Later, as I traveled and studied the Bible more, I changed . . ."

He continued from there, acknowledging his mistakes and affirming that his "pilgrimage" is not yet complete. He talked especially about the arms race, calling for the negotiated destruction of all nuclear weapons.

"I think it's possible," he said. "Maybe not probable, but possible."

In many circles, the speech drew acclaim. Even the daily press, which is customarily myopic about matters of religion, seemed to catch a glimmer of what Graham was driving at. Reporters and editorial writers began dashing off essays about his growth as a Christian—the enlargement of his vision and his definition of sin.

No longer, they noted, did Graham define evil in the world as the debaucheries and excesses of individual people. He had come to see that pervasive social ills—poverty and war and the nuclear arms race—were collective symptoms of the sinful human heart.

Harvard theologian Harvey Cox summed up the sentiments of many of his colleagues when he said with a smile: "I'm very cheered at ol' Billy. He's doing good."

So in a time of great approval from unaccustomed quarters, Graham set out for Moscow. He planned to deliver a speech at an international religious conference on nuclear disarmament, hoping, he said, "to make whatever small contribution I can to the cause of world peace."

But even as he was leaving, an old reluctance showed itself. He fretted with reporters about changes in his image—the publicity about his pleas for disarmament, his passionate denunciations of oppression and hunger. "I don't want to get sidetracked," he said, "and have the press always building me up as the leader of some peace movement."

From the beginning, he seemed unsure and off-stride. And when he confronted tricky subjects—chief among them the Soviet Union's treatment of religious dissidents—he stumbled badly.

He did *not*, as the press widely reported, proclaim that the Soviet Union was a place of religious freedom. But he did say, "I think there is a lot more freedom here than has been given the impression in the United States, because there are hundreds, thousands of churches open." And when a young Baptist woman was led away from one of his speeches, having unfurled a banner denouncing Soviet oppression, Graham defended the police who arrested her.

"Some people can be detained for all kinds of reasons," he said. "We detain people in the United States if we catch people doing things that are wrong. I've had people come to my services in the U.S. causing disturbances, and they have been taken away by police."

Because of such statements, Graham took a battering. Newsweek columnist George Will called him "America's most embarrassing export." Other critics were equally harsh, and in the midst of it all, nobody seemed to remember the original purpose of his trip; nobody seemed to notice that his speech at the conference on nuclear disarmament was one of the most prophetic and powerful ever given on the subject.

At the heart of his message was a quote from Albert Einstein: "The unleashed power of the atom has changed everything except our way of thinking. Thus we are drifting toward a catastrophe beyond comparison. We shall require a substantially new manner of thinking if mankind is to survive."

Graham echoed the sentiment:

"We need a new breakthrough," he declared, "in how the terrifying problem of nuclear war is approached. The vicious cycle of propaganda and counter-propaganda, charge and counter-charge must somehow be broken. The unending and escalating cycle of relying on deterrents should also be defused."

Graham called once again for negotiated arms control, with the ultimate aim of total disarmament. He acknowledged that the process is difficult and far beyond the realms of his own expertise —and so he offered no plan, no concrete proposals for how the negotiations should go.

What he did offer was the ringing conviction that arms negotiations will not succeed, and can *never* succeed, unless we all work to change the climate in which the negotiations occur.

"Our purpose is to rise above narrow national interests," said Graham, "and give all humanity a spiritual vision of the way to peace . . . Let us call the nations and leaders of our world to repentance. We need to repent as nations and over our past failures —the failure to accept each other, the failure to be concerned about the needs of the poor and the starving of the world, the failure to place top priority on peace instead of war . . .

"I would urge the leaders of the nations," he said, "especially the major powers, to declare a moratorium on hostile rhetoric. Peace does not grow in a climate of mistrust, in which each side to a greater and greater degree is constantly accusing the other of false motives and hidden actions."

Throughout the speech and the interviews that surrounded it, Graham insisted that our highly politicized and nationalistic ways of thinking have failed us—that they are attached to a technology where one miscalculation or a single excess of cynicism can lead to Armageddon. And for millions of the world's people, he added, Armageddon is here—for they exist day to day near starvation, while the world's powerful nations, those with the resources to make a dent in suffering, squander billions instead on weapons of mass destruction.

Those are strong words, but most of them were lost in the press reports from Moscow. Still, a few people listened, and it was gratifying to Graham when their praise trickled back. For example, his one-time Baptist antagonist Will Campbell declared after seeing a text of Graham's speeches: "I once accused him of being the court prophet to Richard Nixon. But I have to say, he's God's prophet now."

About the Author

Frye Gaillard is an editorial writer and columnist for the *Charlotte Observer* in Charlotte, N.C. As a reporter, he has covered, among other beats, religion, civil rights and music, winning national and regional awards. He was managing editor of *Race Relations Reporter* magazine, and his by-line has appeared in many national magazines and newspapers, including *Saturday Review, New Times, Us, The Progressive, Newsday* and the *Chicago Tribune*. He was writer-in-residence at Queens College in Charlotte and has lectured at colleges and universities including Vanderbilt, Davidson and the University of South Carolina.

Gaillard grew up in Mobile, Alabama and graduated from Vanderbilt University, where, he says, his racial prejudices and some traditional Southern values—protected through his years at a private, segregated high school—quickly crumbled when exposed to the onslaught of radical ideas surging through universities in the '60s.

While in Nashville Gaillard began meeting country music performers and exploring the relationship of country music to blues and rock 'n' roll and soul. Out of that came his first book, *Watermelon Wine: the Spirit of Country Music,* widely acclaimed for its clarity and insight into the country music world. It was one of 300 books selected in 1979 to go to Moscow for the International Book Fair, sponsored by the Association of American Publishers. The exhibit, "America through American Eyes," showed books representative of contemporary American life.

Today Gaillard describes himself as a Southern junkie: sometimes chauvinist, sometimes voyeur, sometimes bleeding-heart critic. As he writes about the South and its people, he adroitly avoids both the condescension outsiders often display in commenting on the South and the defensiveness that can still prevail when Southerners write about themselves. With a critical mind and a generous heart, he weaves together the journalist's close observation of detail and the historian's eye for the trends and issues that shape our times.

Photo Credits

Page 34, by Tom Franklin, *Charlotte News*

Pages 39, 86 by Steve Perille, *Charlotte Observer*

Pages 78, 166 (bottom) by Mark B. Sluder, *Charlotte Observer*

Page 96 by Gary Parker, *Charlotte Observer*

Pages 113, 115 by Elmer Horton, *Charlotte News*

Pages 122, 141 by Phil Drake, *Charlotte Observer*

Page 157 by Don Hunter, *Charlotte News*

Page 162 (top) by Don Sturkey, *Charlotte Observer*

"For a young journalist still in his thirties, Frye Gaillard has already had a notable and prolific career. Over the past 17 years, he has written hundreds of stories for more than a score of newspapers and magazines.

"Gaillard writes with a wisdom beyond his years. Though he could be considered a latecomer, in a chronological sense, to the three themes of this book—Southern race relations, music and religion—he handles these complex subjects with sure-handed knowledge, skill and confidence. Frye Gaillard has written like a seasoned veteran almost from the start of his career—and as this collection of some of his pieces clearly shows, he is blooming now more impressively than ever."

—John Egerton,
author of *The Americanization of Dixie*

"Frye Gaillard is a good and honest and inquiring man. He is of that generation of Southerners who bothered, for the first time, to ask questions. He is a first-rate journalist who heard the answers."

—Paul Hemphill,
author of *The Good Old Boys*

"In a rare stroke of creative journalism, Frye Gaillard has tied together three topics which go to the heart of the American character and experience. This is a balanced treatment of a complex set of inter-relationships and, as far as I know, is unique in American journalism."

—Billy O. Wireman,
President, Queens College

"Writing with the polite sensitivity, measured rhythms and graceful seductiveness of the region which spawned him, Frye Gaillard instinctively homes in on the paradox and tragedy which define the Southern character. Excellent journalism."

—Doug Marlette,
nationally syndicated cartoonist

East Woods Press Books

Backcountry Cooking
Berkshire Trails for Walking & Ski Touring
Campfire Chillers
Canoeing the Jersey Pine Barrens
Carolina Seashells
Carpentry: Some Tricks of the Trade from an Old-Style Carpenter
Catfish Cookbook, The
Complete Guide to Backpacking in Canada
Drafting: Tips and Tricks on Drawing and Designing House Plans
Exploring Nova Scotia
Free Attractions, USA
Free Campgrounds, USA
Fructose Cookbook, The
Grand Strand: An Uncommon Guide to Myrtle Beach, The
Healthy Trail Food Book, The
Hiking from Inn to Inn
Hiking Virginia's National Forests
Honky Tonkin': Travel Guide to American Music
Hosteling USA, Revised Edition
Inside Outward Bound
Interior Finish: More Tricks of the Trade
    from an Old-Style Carpenter
Just Folks: Visitin' with Carolina People
Kays Gary, Columnist
Living Land: An Outdoor Guide to North Carolina, The
Making Food Beautiful
Maine Coast: A Nature Lover's Guide, The
New England Guest House Book, The
New England: Off the Beaten Path
Parent Power!
    A Common-Sense Approach to Raising Your Children In The Eighties
Race, Rock and Religion
Rocky Mountain National Park Hiking Trails
Sea Islands of the South
Southern Guest House Book, The
Southern Rock: A Climber's Guide to the South
Steppin' Out: A Guide to Live Music in Manhattan
Sweets Without Guilt
Tennessee Trails
Train Trips: Exploring America by Rail
Trout Fishing the Southern Appalachians
Vacationer's Guide to Orlando and Central Florida, A
Walks in the Catskills
Walks in the Great Smokies
Walks with Nature in Rocky Mountain National Park
Whitewater Rafting in Eastern America
Wild Places of the South
Woman's Journey, A
You Can't Live on Radishes

Order from:
The East Woods Press
429 East Blvd.
Charlotte, NC 28203